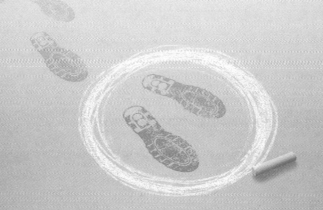

ONE1CRY

A Nationwide Call for Spiritual Awakening

BYRON PAULUS & BILL ELLIFF

MOODY PUBLISHERS
CHICAGO

All Scripture quotations, unless otherwise indicated, are taken from the *New American Standard Bible*®, Copyright © 1960, 1962, 1963, 1968, 1971, 1972, 1973, 1975, 1977, 1995 by The Lockman Foundation. Used by permission. (www.Lockman.org)

Scripture quotations marked ESV are taken from *The Holy Bible, English Standard Version*. Copyright © 2000, 2001 by Crossway Bibles, a division of Good News Publishers. Used by permission. All rights reserved.

Scripture quotations marked NIV are taken from the *Holy Bible, New International Version*®, NIV®. Copyright ©1973, 1978, 1984, 2011 by Biblica, Inc.™ Used by permission of Zondervan. All rights reserved worldwide. www.zondervan.com

Scripture quotations marked NLT are taken from the *Holy Bible, New Living Translation*, copyright © 1996, 2004. Used by permission of Tyndale House Publishers, Inc., Wheaton, Illinois 60189, U.S.A. All rights reserved.

All added emphasis in Scripture citations comes from the authors.

Edited by Elizabeth Cody Newenhuyse
Interior and cover design: Design Corps
Cover images: iStockphoto.com: #23475910 / # 22588366 / # 19575299
Author photo: Bill Elliff-Kyle Uptergrove

Library of Congress Cataloging-in-Publication Data

Paulus, Byron.
  OneCry : a nationwide call for spiritual awakening / Byron Paulus, Bill Elliff.
    pages cm
  Includes bibliographical references.
  ISBN 978-0-8024-1139-6
  1. Christianity—United States—21st century. 2. Church renewal—United States. 3. Religious awakening—United States. 4. Revivals—United States. I. Title. II. Title: One cry.
  BR526.P38 2014
  269—dc23

                                              2013039479

All websites listed herein are accurate at the time of publication but may change in the future or cease to exist. The listing of website references and resources does not imply publisher endorsement of the site's entire contents. Groups and organizations are listed for informational purposes, and listing does not imply publisher endorsement of their activities.

We hope you enjoy this book from Moody Publishers. Our goal is to provide high-quality, thought-provoking books and products that connect truth to your real needs and challenges. For more information on other books and products written and produced from a biblical perspective, go to www.moodypublishers.com or write to:

Moody Publishers
820 N. LaSalle Boulevard
Chicago, IL 60610

5 7 9 10 8 6 4

Printed in the United States of America

ABOUT THE COVER:
Let It Begin in Me

The cover pictures a critical spiritual principle: Revival begins in the heart of anyone *willing to confess their need for God and cry out for His power and activity in their life. We all have a tendency to focus on the needs of others, but God wants us to start with ourselves. Will you be one who* steps into the circle of personal authenticity *before God and prays, "Lord, please begin Your work in me today!"*

Contents

ONECRY
ACROSS THE NATION

*A*cross *the nation, leaders of all ages are joining their voices for God to send sweeping revival and spiritual awakening.* Their cries can be heard emanating from north, south, east, and west. They know no denominational or racial divides. No economic or gender barriers. These sacred prayers reflect the deepest heart-longings of thousands in the body of Christ today. May God hear and answer with manifest power for Jesus' sake!

> *Father, as we look at the church of Laodicea, we are reminded that Jesus was outside the door of the church. Father, we invite Jesus back in. Come back in, Jesus, and take over our congregations, and show us Your glory.*
>
> **Erwin Lutzer**
> Senior Pastor, The Moody Church
> Speaker/Author, *When a Nation Forgets God*

> *We're praying and we're dreaming along with the believers all around America, asking for a revival in this next generation. As we've seen throughout history, God loves to use young people—young men and young women to repaint the face of Jesus and Christianity to an entire culture.*
>
> **Nick Hall**
> Founder/Evangelist, PULSE, Minneapolis, MN

> *I pray that there would be a revival in our love for You, Lord, and that that'll translate into action. If we love things in this world too much, would You just open our eyes to that or even take them away from us, Lord, so that You again will be our first love?*
>
> **Francis Chan**
> Founding Pastor, Cornerstone Church, Simi Valley, CA
> Speaker/Author, *Crazy Love*

7

*Lord, if we have true revival, we're going to see the walls and
the barriers of denominations and race and creed and prejudice
all broken down in a way that sweeps through our lives and our
churches. And I pray that it would happen, in Jesus' name.*

Michael Catt
Senior Pastor, Sherwood Baptist Church, Albany, GA
Executive Producer, *Facing the Giants, Fireproof, Courageous*
Founder, ReFRESH Revival Conference

*I pray that You would help us to realize that our identity in Christ is more
important than our ethnicity or any other way that we identify ourselves,
and that it's our position in the body of Christ that makes us one.*

Daniel Simmons
Senior Pastor, Mount Zion Baptist Church, Albany, GA

*Father, God, I pray that You would just help us as a body throughout
the nation and around the world to come to that place where we
recognize that our commonality is in Christ Jesus and Christ Jesus
alone. I pray we will come to that place where we will set aside all of
our logos and lift up the Logos, the Word of God.*

Gary Frost
Vice President, Midwest Region and Prayer
North American Mission Board (SBC)

*Lord God, we need to find our identity in You, not in our struggle, not in
our sexuality, not in our race, not in our gender, Lord God, but we need
to find our identity in You, O God, and that is how revival will come.*

Christopher Yuan
Author/Speaker/Teacher, Chicago, IL

*We pray, God, that You would do things that are bigger than we could
ever imagine. We're asking things to happen in churches all across this
nation that have nothing to do with personality of the preacher. We ask
that Your Word would be lifted up high, that Your Spirit would flow
freely. God, do Your work; do things that surprise us. In Jesus' name.*

Gregg Matte
Senior Pastor, First Baptist Church, Houston, TX

Father, we ask that You would do something so great in this country that it would take our collective spiritual breath away. Oh God, do something unimaginable—beyond anything that we've ever seen. We don't seek for an experience, just the transformation of lives so that all will stand back and say, "Look at God!"

Crawford Loritts
Senior Pastor, Fellowship Baptist Church, Roswell, GA
Author/Speaker/Host, *Living a Legacy*

Father, we are indifferent. We are apathetic. We talk about revival. We desire revival. We preach about revival. We study revival. Yet, Lord, we don't experience it within our heart because of that sense of spiritual coma, that doubt that is there, because of sin and pride and an unbroken heart.

Dick Eastman
International President of Every Home for Christ
President, America's National Prayer Committee
Author/Originator, *Change the World School of Prayer*

Father, we know that revival is a sovereign work from Your hand and Your hand alone. We pray that You would have mercy on Your bride. Restore us. Bless us. Heal us, that we would love one another. Father, we cry out for mercy.

Fern Nichols
Founder/President, Moms in Prayer International
Author/Speaker

God, I pray for a revival among the men of America. I thank You for the prayer groups of women that I've heard about and, yet, Father, the men fall so far short and follow so far behind. I pray God that You would raise up men who seek You, men who put You first.

Sammy Tippit
Evangelist/Revivalist, Sammy Tippit Ministries
San Antonio, TX

We ask in Your mighty name and in Your mighty power, to move in the direction that You desire, to bring reconciliation and renewal leading to revival. We know You can do it, so we ask You, Holy Spirit. Would You do this, Father? Would You convict across the nation of anything we do to get in Your way?

Jeremy Story
President, Campus Renewal Ministries, New York, NY

Father, open the windows of heaven and come down and bless Your church across the land. We are so absolutely helpless without Your Holy Spirit. We have nothing. There is nothing in our hands that we can do because we have nothing unless You give it to us. So we plead with You today. Open the windows of heaven and pour out a blessing. Make us open as never before and helpless and desperate for the movement and power of Your Holy Spirit. Help us not to depend on our talent, our ability, our intelligence, our cleverness; but help us to be wide open to You—not only wide open to others and honest with them, but wide open to You.

Jim Cymbala
Senior Pastor, The Brooklyn Tabernacle, Brooklyn, NY
Author/Speaker

We need a cleansing, Lord, and we pray that Your Holy Spirit would sweep across this nation, beginning with the church and then with homes and then with our government leaders; Lord, that we all might be drawn to You, that we all might be a holy bride to You. I feel like we should put on sackcloth and throw ashes on our head and lie prostrate before You and cry out for the sins of our nation. We thank You for Your mercy, and we thank You for Your compassion. We thank You for Your steadfast love. In Christ's name.

Shirley Dobson
Chair, National Day of Prayer Task Force

God, we come together, having knit our hearts with thanksgiving. Lord, You're grieved, deeply grieved over our hearts, our lives, our church, our nation, our need, and the need of people around the world; yet we are excited, Lord, by this wonderful truth, that we can be filled with Your Spirit. Fill us with Your life.

Tom Elliff
President, International Mission Board (SBC)

O God, when we are too well pleased with ourselves, when our dreams come true simply because we have dreamed too little, when we arrive safely simply because we have sailed too close to the shore, push back the horizons of our hope, help us to see humankind as You see it, and move us in to a future, O Holy One, fueled by faith, focus, and fortitude.

Barry Black
62nd Chaplain, US Senate
Retired Rear Admiral/Chief of Navy Chaplains

God made a historical, eternal promise to us when He said, If My people who are called by My Name would humble themselves and pray and then turn from their wicked ways, then God said that He would hear us from heaven, He would forgive our sins, and He would heal our land, and that we would return to Him, and He says that I'll return to you. And so this is a crucial time in our nation, and oh that we would see that renewal that comes from You.

John Perkins
International Author/Speaker/Lecturer
President Emeritus, John M. Perkins Foundation
for Reconciliation and Development

Lord, revival is what You want to send. God, we pray that You would stir up our spirits, that You would find us faithful, and that You would find us on our knees because we know that when we get on our knees, You extend Your powerful right hand.

Mark Batterson
Lead Pastor, National Community Church
Washington, D.C.

11

Lord, we see in our land the intensifying battle between good and evil—between heaven and hell. Oh God, as we see the flood of evil coming in through the values and lifestyles, and the anti-Christian efforts made on the part of a dedicated handful, we pray that You would raise up a standard of righteousness against the enemy. We pray that You would move in and through Your people to raise up in this land a God-consciousness—a fear of the Lord.

Nancy Leigh DeMoss
Teacher/Author/Speaker; Host of *Revive Our Hearts*

Father, there are so many different sins that we need to confess to You: materialism, and consumerism, and racism, and all of the things that we've done because we have not sought Your face, we have not sought Your ways, we have not sought first Your kingdom. And so we come to You and we humble ourselves. You have told us that You oppose the proud but give grace to the humble. We humble ourselves before You. We need Your cleansing.

Rick Warren
Pastor, Saddleback Church, Lake Forest, CA

Our gracious Heavenly Father, we want our hearts to burn. We want real revival, but we cannot ever pray for revival without asking for repentance. So, God, draw us to the chalk circle. Draw us to that moment of private prayer like evangelist Gypsy Smith said. Move in our hearts, cause us to do housecleaning, deep housecleaning where we're willing to identify the sin that so easily entangles. Father, You are issuing a wake-up call, and we tremble because You are a holy God. We take comfort in knowing that You are a God of love. But we recognize, Father, that time is running out. Even so, come, Lord Jesus.

Janet Parshall
Author/Radio Host, "In the Market with Janet Parshall"

DEDICATION

To those who have never seen but always hoped. Never experienced but always believed. Tasted but longed for more. These men have modeled the passion and lived the commitment that we desire. They have paved a highway for us to travel as we seek the Lord's face.

Thank you, Heavenly Father, for allowing our hearts to be touched and transformed by these godly revival leaders. Much of what the OneCry movement embodies today is the fruit of their labor.

Del Fehsenfeld Jr. (1947–1989)
"As long as God is on His throne, revival is as possible as the sun rising tomorrow morning."

Leonard Ravenhill (1907–1994)
"If we are content to live without revival, we will."

Bill McLeod (1918–2012)
"In times of evangelism, evangelists seek sinners. But in times of revival, sinners seek the Lord!"

J. Edwin Orr (1912–1987)
"We've learned enough to know He will come, but have we learned enough to pray until He does?"

FOREWORD

My friend Byron Paulus lives with one main passion: to see the church of Jesus Christ experience a true spiritual revival. OneCry, the movement God birthed in Byron's heart, rightly asserts that unless the people belonging to God humble themselves and call to Him for a visitation of His Holy Spirit, there is no hope for America. The only answer to the sin problem of men and women today is Jesus Christ, and who can powerfully share the gospel but a spiritually awakened and reinvigorated church?

God has chosen not to use angels or His omnipotence to turn the tide here on earth. Instead He has sovereignly chosen to use believing Christians as His instruments of redemption in a lost world. But can a sleeping, lackadaisical church accomplish this task?

The church must be revived not merely to have revival but, rather, that in God's strength, she can carry out Christ's mission to seek and save that which is lost. OneCry reminds us that the revival we all need will come only through humble repentance and fervent prayer filled with faith that God *will* do what He promised.

The heart of OneCry is powerfully expressed in a "Declaration of National Spiritual Emergency." I vividly remember the first time I heard the words of this declaration in a gathering with hundreds of other pastors, including Bill Elliff who co-authored this book. My heart resonated with the declaration's clarion call to turn in humble repentance from sin, to God in fervent prayer, and to unity with other believers in solidarity to share this message with others. Hundreds of us signed this declaration, pledging ourselves to this cry for revival, and I encourage you to do the same (see the declaration on page 130).

The Laodicean church that Christ wrote to (Revelation 3) was a Christian church and members of His covenant people. In his letter, Jesus never mentions one word of false doctrine or teaching that had invaded the church. Yet Christ reveals to them that He is on the outside, knocking at the door to enter His own church! Only an invasion of God's Spirit can cure us from the Laodicean lukewarmness Jesus condemned. It is all around us, and the only answer is the fire of His Presence descending upon us as we plead for more of Him.

OneCry: A Nationwide Call for Spiritual Awakening, if read with an open heart, will stir you to be a part of the army of intercessors God is raising up to pray down the breakthrough we need. And it will urge pastors across this nation to preach and proclaim the hope of Christ-centered revival in their churches.

You will never be the same once the hunger for spiritual renewal is birthed in your heart by God Himself. Read this book. Pray its prayers. Let it inspire you to share the hope of revival and spiritual awakening with others. And then let us watch for God to come to revive His people.

Jim Cymbala

Watch the Declaration of National Spiritual Emergency video and digitally sign the Declaration online at www.OneCry.com.

BEFORE YOU STEP IN . . .

This book gives voice to a surging movement of diverse Jesus-followers who recognize the profound brokenness in lives, families, churches, and communities all around us. But even more importantly, it embraces the hope that God powerfully delivers and restores people who cry out to Him in repentance, prayer, and collective obedience. These convictions are the foundation of the *one cry* that is encouraged throughout this book.

OneCry is best summarized by a core document called "The Declaration of National Spiritual Emergency." Although the Declaration does not appear until page 130, the substance and spirit of it is fleshed out on every page, and you may wish to read it first as a guidepost for the rest of the book.

The aim of OneCry is to catalyze a resurgence of Christ-followers of every stripe (denominationally, ethnically, generationally, and geographically) who will unite in biblical repentance and fervent prayer for the extraordinary work of the Holy Spirit in our day.

Toward that end, there are several features of this book that have been designed to turn what you read into an encounter with God, whether you read it alone or with a small group. And our goal throughout is to provide opportunities for you to share what impacts you with others:

1. Making It Personal — Each of the chapters ends with a *Thinking It Through* exercise to personalize application of the truths presented, as well as a *Crying Out!* section to turn the focus to prayer. Answering the questions and engaging in prayer is one way to ensure you are stepping into the circle of revival.

2. Individual / Small Group Video & Resources — Byron and Bill have created short video introductions for each chapter that are perfect for getting your small group ready to discuss the truths presented in each chapter. And if you are walking through this study alone, it will be equally helpful. These videos have been posted online where small group leaders will also find a downloadable guide and a host of supplementary material for each chapter.

3. Going Deeper at OneCryBook.com — Each chapter ends with a "Quick Response" (QR) code that leads you to additional resources, taking you deeper into the topic. Easily accessible online and categorized by chapter, these resources have been carefully selected based on over four decades of revival ministry, and have a proven track record of effectiveness with thousands of people.

4. #OneCry — To make sharing the message of OneCry simple, short quotes will be highlighted for Twitter, Facebook, or other social media platforms. And if you don't want to go to the effort of retyping them on your computer or mobile device, they have been catalogued online and linked to various forms of social media for push-button ease of use.

5. Pastors — Companion resources have been created to help make the *OneCry* book an eight-week, concentrated, *whole church* experience. Suggested worship themes, small group videos, discussion guides, and sermon helps will enable your people to gain an understanding of the history of revival, its biblical basis, and practical steps they can take towards experiencing revival and spiritual awakening. A church kit, available at www.OneCryBook.com/churchkit, will include:

- Small Group Leader's guide, discussion questions, and teaching videos.
- Pastors' resources include sermon starters, PowerPoint templates, and teaching resources.
- Church promotional resources and guides on how to lead OneCry in a local church setting.

Finally, a few words about the way this book is organized: *think of this book as a journey to revival.*

In Part One, Byron Paulus, the founder of the OneCry movement, provides an "on ramp" to the OneCry highway, explaining why this particular trip could be the most important and most exciting you have ever taken.

In Part Two, Bill Elliff picks up as an experienced and wise guide, providing six powerful realities for how to experience revival personally and corporately.

And in closing, Byron returns in Part Three to help you exit into your daily life, activating the truths you have learned, while inviting you to mobilize with thousands of others in the wider OneCry movement.

It is our prayer that somewhere along the way, you will truly step into the revolutionary hope of revival.

PART ONE

WHY ONECRY?

Indelibly etched in my (Byron's) memory are a number of agonizing cries. As a teenager, I will never forget the heartbreaking cry of my mother as I watched two army officers approach the back door of our farmhouse to tell our family about the death of my older brother in Vietnam. That piercing cry still echoes in my heart.

As a husband, my own cry joined my wife Sue's when we found out the heartbeat of our unborn child had ceased. At the gravesite, our united cries expressed our deep sense of loss.

On other occasions, my cries have been with and for the suffering of dear friends. In one instance, I was on the phone with one of my staff when I heard the scream of his wife in the background as their infant daughter breathed her last breath, losing her battle with leukemia.

A fallen soldier, a deceased infant, a bereaved mother.

Have you ever experienced a deep, heartrending cry?

It's Time to Cry *UP*

But crying out is not always the same thing as crying up. Sometimes our cries are born out of anger—cries *at* or cries *for* or cries *because*. But OneCry goes beyond those kinds of cries.

OneCry is about a *vertical* cry. Like the cry of Moses when he asked God to spare the nation from destruction. Or when the Israelites came together to grieve after the ark of God had been stolen and the nation had lost the glory of God. Like the cry of Psalm 85, when broken hearts looked toward heaven and pleaded, "Will you not revive us again, that your people may rejoice in you?" (v. 6 ESV). Or when Isaiah cried with prophetic passion, "Oh, that you would

23

burst forth from the heavens and come down!" (Isaiah 64:1 NLT).

CRYING OUT IS NOT ALWAYS THE SAME THING AS *CRYING UP.*

A vertical cry is not always a corporate cry for a beleaguered nation, a hurting community, a lifeless church, or even a messed-up family. Sometimes it is a very personal cry erupting from a deep spiritual need. And that is where it must begin, in the circle of our own heart. Like the stories that follow of David and Diane and thousands more in our nation who cannot stop crying over the condition of their own troubled soul:

God found me hard and closed off. Hurtful words, harsh actions, and bitter attitudes had so caused deep wounds in my heart that I shut down. I didn't want to pray any more, sing any more, fellowship any more. I had come to a place of "why bother?" I became the very person I had been hurt by. I wanted to hurt instead of being hurt. God created such anguish in my heart that I literally could not breathe. I begged and cried out for God to show me what was wrong. Through the Scriptures God spoke to me that He is my mighty warrior, and He will deal with my hurts if I let Him. I listed them specifically and, praise the Lord, I gave them all to Him that night. I am free! – David

Today I went to my knees before God to confess all that my broken heart could reveal and to remove the mask covering my heart. I asked a godly person to pray with me. For the first time, God gave me grace and strength to be as broken as an open acorn, to open my heart to let the old life flee and the courage to rebuild my life. I cried out to God, then I cried and cried some more, and prayed like never before. I feel that God has truly changed me! – Diane

God found me not only broke but completely shattered. I was a

truly pathetic mess for years. Rape, thoughts of suicide, pot and alcohol abuse, and self-inflicting harm. I was ashamed of all that and more. I tried my hardest to deal with it on my own. How would my parents be able to face the church if their own daughter wasn't leaning on God for her problems? My father, a pastor, shouldn't have a daughter doing those things. I called upon God when He had about 33 percent of me. Now, I'm all His. I am slowly telling my parents, and without the passion I now have for God, I wouldn't be able to do anything. I can't do it alone. I never should have tried. – Allison

Twelve years ago, I came face-to-face with death. On the way home from a college mission trip, our plane crash-landed in a severe thunderstorm, killing eleven people, including two of my friends sitting next to me. I walked away almost unscathed, but I would carry emotional scars with me for years to come. Where was God when my friends needed Him? And why did He choose to spare my life? It took four years of counseling, but I finally let go of my anger against God. I learned to pray earnestly again. I even learned to trust Him when I started flying again. – Harold

No matter how difficult or hopeless of a situation we find ourselves in, God is waiting for our cry. OneCry is the cry of the soul that longs for God to come in all His glory.

A Sacred Cry

Have you ever been so swept up in the purposes of God, the lostness of the world, the brokenness of your own condition, the desire for Christ's honor, that you lifted your eyes to heaven and wept? Have your tears for His kingdom to come ever rivaled agonizing human cries of despair or bondage or sorrow?

This kind of heartfelt, passionate cry, this anguish of soul, is what it means to seek God fervently.[1] It is this kind of cry we hear Jesus pouring forth when He wept over the city of Jerusalem. It is also reflected in the intensity of the cry of Jesus in the garden of Gethsemane (Luke 19:41; Hebrews 5:7). And as Jesus experienced, seeking God earnestly may require great personal sacrifice.

But some things are so important that they are worth the cost. And once we see the value of the power and presence of God as well as the alternatives without Him, I believe we will cry out to God like never before.

In fact, the cry of a God-seeker is not a morbid, defeated cry. *It is a cry of hope.* A cry that looks to heaven and changes the way we live on earth. A cry that resets priorities and rearranges schedules. A cry that will turn you from a prayer spectator to a prayer warrior. A cry that will take you to places you've never imagined and demand sacrifices on a level you never anticipated, but will also cause you to love and live more like Christ than you ever thought possible.

THE CRY OF A GOD-SEEKER IS NOT A MORBID, DEFEATED CRY. IT IS A CRY OF HOPE.

This cry, this one cry, is a turnaround moment. It's a moment when we admit that we don't have the answers. We don't have solutions. We can't fix what's broken in our world. Our one cry upward to God, born in humility, is our ultimate admission of need before Him. And when we admit our need, when we humble ourselves before the Lord, He gives grace. And everything changes. Not because of us, but because of Him.

We cry up to God in that sacred moment when we realize we have nothing else to offer.

Hidden Danger

When the I-35 bridge collapsed in Minneapolis a number of years ago, sending sixty cars careening down into the Mississippi River, speculation regarding the cause started almost immediately.

It soon became clear that the problem wasn't simply a matter of external stressors. The collapse came from within, due to structural problems that were not readily apparent. In strategic areas, the metal supports slowly became "fatigued." After decades of heavy use, the bridge finally could no longer bear the weight.

Sadly, after the crash, an investigation revealed that even though the bridge had been declared deficient by government inspectors, the serious work of overhaul was never prioritized. Restorative measures would have required shutting down the highway, rerouting traffic for months, and taking time to lift the entire structure in order to get to problems beneath the surface of the river.

Doing what it took to address the real issues was deemed too difficult. Too time consuming. Too costly. No one was willing to make the necessary adjustments to do what was needed to avoid disaster. Band-Aids were used when a total overhaul was required.

I wonder if America is in just as precarious a position today? Could business as usual be keeping us from taking seriously the dangers facing our society? Or, as in Minneapolis, perhaps the issues have been duly noted, but few are willing to do what's necessary to go below the surface to the heart of the problems. The "heavenly inspector" says, "Fix it," and we reply, "It doesn't fit in our schedules. It's too inconvenient. It won't be popular. It costs too much."

But how much longer can our nation bear the weight? Tomorrow may be too late.

Warning Signs

The Bible warns us to take action before it becomes too late: "Today when you hear [God's] voice, don't harden your hearts as Israel did when they rebelled" (Hebrews 3:15 NLT). The foundation of any nation is found in the hearts of its people. "If the foundations are destroyed, what can the righteous do?" (Psalm 11:3 ESV).

Warning signs that America has heart trouble are everywhere, aren't they? Financially, we are facing crushing debt and abiding fear of economic meltdown. Sociologically, our families are splitting up and being redefined by cohabitation, divorce, and so-called same-sex marriage. Educationally, many schools are failing and our kids are falling behind other developed countries. Politically, we are divided and gridlocked while facing new kinds of global threats.

At some level, the message is sinking in. Polls show that most Americans agree that the country is on the wrong track. Something is desperately wrong, and we know it. But just how bad is it? What it the extent of the problems we face?

There is ample statistical evidence that it is not well in the United States (or in the rest of Western Civilization, for that matter). Yet I fear that such statistics have become so familiar to us that we've begun to accept their conclusions as "normal." But they aren't! Our nation shouldn't be defined by . . .

Fatherlessness. There are more unmarried mothers under age 30 than married mothers, with 40% of all babies born out of wedlock, and 48% of all first births to unmarried women.[2]

Imprisonment. More than 7 million adults are on probation, on parole, in jail or prison—the most of any nation on earth.[3]

Perversion. 40 million visitors peruse porn sites on the web—with the average age of first visits being age 11. And the most religious states (the Bible Belt) have the highest percentage![4]

Culture of Death. Since 1973, the total number of American lives lost to abortion is roughly equal to the collective world-wide death toll of World War II (approximately 60 million souls).

Chaos and Confusion. Biblical cultural standards have been jettisoned by government, the media, and a significant portion of the U.S. population (even within the church).

Bondage. America's national debt continues to grow, and in the future we face $124 trillion in unfunded liabilities—more than the *world's* GDP (83 trillion) and over $1,000,000 per U.S. taxpayer. And, this reality says nothing about the lifestyle of personal indebtedness that plagues many U.S. families.[5]

And stats do not tell the whole story because behind every stat is a personal experience. After forty years of ministry in over 6,000 local churches across America, I continue to hear the stories of this disintegration every day. And the *personal cost* of having lost our way is overwhelming.

Every year, I receive thousands of letters from people who have encountered God in personal spiritual revival. But it's not the number of respondents I find significant as much as the depth of pain and dysfunction they have endured before experiencing God's intervention.

Here are a few examples of recent letters. I narrowed this sample to women, and then further narrowed it to women who were connected to church leadership.

- My sister-in-law is divorcing her husband and leaving her three boys to marry her former pastor. We grieve over this as a Christian family.

- My husband was once a pastor. He is now very worldly minded and disillusioned. This has been hard for our marriage.

- My pastor-husband left me for his secretary. The divorce was finalized two weeks ago. Pray for restoration to God and family.

- My sister has left her husband and believes she is in love with her pastor. Both families are in the midst of divorce and planning their new life together.

- There is a man I *hate*. He ran my father who's a pastor off from his church. I need to release my anger and hate.

These needy people are not alone. And if this is occurring in the pulpits of our land, imagine what is happening in the pew. Could this simply be the tip of the iceberg representing the havoc that broken lives, broken families, broken churches, and a broken society have left in its wake?

They are all casualties of the spiritual battle that is raging in our nation at this very moment. And every day, lives are swept away in a sea of hopelessness, bitterness, and confusion.

Empty lives. Broken families. A disintegrating nation. Like the I-35 bridge in Minneapolis, external pressure is mounting while the support mechanisms are increasingly fatigued and unable to support the weight.

That's where we find ourselves. And, unfortunately, there's nothing on the horizon that can or will change any of that. Look to the east, the north, the south, and the west. There are no human answers.

A State of Emergency

A chorus of voices from all sectors of our society has begun to sound an alarm. The trajectory of America on many levels is unsustainable economically, socially, politically, and morally.

This unsustainable course can't be fixed by rearranging government programs or implementing new policies. It isn't ultimately about combating violence or cleaning up the streets or even protesting the evils of society. No, the answer is spiritual. The answer is to call out for God's mercy, for the hope and transformation that only He can bring to a prodigal nation.

Is it possible then that the greatest threat America faces may be God Himself as He withholds His mercy and exercises His righteous judgment?

Consider these words from the heart of God to the nations:

If at any time I announce that a nation or kingdom is to be uprooted, torn down and destroyed, and if that nation I warned repents of its evil, then I will relent and not inflict on it the disaster I had planned. And if at another time I announce that a nation or kingdom is to be built up and planted, and if it does evil in my sight and does not obey me, then I will reconsider the good I had intended to do for it.
(Jeremiah 18:7–10 NIV)

The principle in these verses is undeniable—God not only blesses people and nations, He judges them as well.

As Dr. Erwin Lutzer puts it, "The God of the Bible will not endlessly tolerate idolatry and benign neglect. He graciously endures rejection and insults, but at some point, He might choose to bring a nation to its knees with severe discipline."[6]

So how urgent are the days in which we live? Scholar and revival historian Richard Owen Roberts writes:

> *When the people of God sin against Him and do not repent, He judges them. While some of these judgments are final and consist of death and destruction, the more standard form of judgment is both remedial and gracious and consists of withdrawal of certain evidences of His manifest presence and merciful favors. In the absence of God's manifest presence, there is always an immediate and extensive increase in iniquity. . . . **God has judged America with the remedial judgment of withdrawal of certain manifestations of His gracious presence and mercy.*** [emphasis added][7]

The painful effects of wickedness we are experiencing—in our families, in our communities, even in our government—all of this showcases how much we need God's grace.

America is in a state of spiritual emergency. It's not just because of how the world is acting, but how the church is behaving. Where does judgment begin, after all, if not in the house of God (1 Peter 4:17)?

How we respond to our current trajectory will determine our ultimate outcome. It's time to cry up, to utter a desperate cry to God before it's too late.

The Cry That Counts

A number of years ago, I visited our nation's capital. While there for meetings, I had gone to the office of a US Senator to pray for him. Having just left, I found myself standing halfway between the US Supreme Court building and the US Capitol, two magnificent buildings representing two powerful branches of our government. That's when my cellphone rang.

It was a dear Christian friend whose teenage daughter had just confessed to him of having lost her virginity with a man she had just met. Devastated, this father was asking if he could fly to Washington D.C. that night to meet me.

I was shocked. My wife and I had spent many hours investing in this young woman's life. She was a vibrant Christian who had surrendered her life to full-time vocational ministry, and now *this?*

As I hung up the phone, tears filled my eyes and I became exasperated. I looked at the Capitol and thought, "If our legislature would just make better laws, this type of thing would never happen! Our culture is filled with evil and it is allowed to run rampant through every corner, and our elected officials won't do anything to stop it. Our young people don't stand a chance!"

Then as I turned, I noticed the Supreme Court building, and I hurled more accusations: "If our courts would just interpret the law instead of making new laws to conform to our lifestyle, succumbing to what the people want as a license to live wicked lives, this would never happen!"

But then the Lord pressed something distinctly in my heart— it was as if God was opening my eyes to something significant to Him: "Byron, you are standing in the *wrong place*. You are blaming the *wrong people*."

Later that night, I went to the book of Joel where a determined prophet spoke with certainty as he confronted the darkness of his day: "Between the vestibule and the altar let the priests, the ministers of the Lord, weep . . ." (Joel 2:17 ESV). The location is significant in this passage. Joel is urging the spiritual leaders of his day to weep between the people of God (the vestibule) and the presence of God (the altar).

I realized God was impressing something important on me that night. The solution for the moral, social, and economic problems in our culture will ultimately never be found in Washington.

I needed to look where God looks—at the condition of His people and His church.

As Leonard Ravenhill once put it, "The church is waiting for the world to become regenerate, while the world is waiting for the church to become repentant."

Erwin Lutzer makes a similar point: "Perhaps the church doesn't suffer for the sins of the world as much as the world suffers for the sins of the church."

It is clear the repentant cry of God's people is the cry that moves them toward His presence.

The extraordinary thing that God does in response to the repentant cries of His people is called revival and spiritual awakening.

> **THE REPENTANT CRY OF GOD'S PEOPLE IS THE CRY THAT MOVES THEM TOWARD HIS PRESENCE.**

The Power of an Upward Cry

When God comes in revival, He accomplishes in a brief time what would normally take many years. Revival is the intensifying, accelerating, multiplying, and magnifying work of God. This does not diminish the value of the normal means and timing of God, but rather highlights the importance of seeking those divine seasons of God's extraordinary flow of grace.

That's why the patriarchs, the prophets, the disciples, the apostles, and the early church fathers were always seeking a greater measure of God's presence. They realized that without God's manifest presence, little of eternal significance would transpire. Knowing how desperately they needed God, they were set on seeking Him.

And, historically, great men and women of God have realized their great need for God's presence to do His great work, and thus, the pursuit of revival and spiritual awakening became their passion. Before the twentieth century, the United States experienced at least three sweeping movements of God's Spirit—periods historians call Great Awakenings.

What happens during massive movements of the Spirit of God will be the subject of the next chapter, but the impact is staggering. In short, when spiritual awakening takes place, the advance of the gospel speeds up dramatically. What seemed impossible suddenly unfolds. Revival is an extraordinary movement of the Spirit of God that produces extraordinary results.

But is spiritual awakening merely a relic of a bygone era? Or could it really happen in our day?

Not in a Million Years!

It was a dreary and gray day in the former Communist country. The clouds overhead resembled the thick clouds that, for a century, overshadowed any hope that Communist Romania would one day be free. The idea that any nation this repressed would experience a complete shift from hardline Communism to full-fledged democracy and religious freedom was far-fetched at best.

The conversation I had with Florine, a young Romanian pastor, confirmed how densely thick those clouds really were. We had just crossed the border from Hungary into Romania when I felt the timing was right to ask.

I could tell it was still raw for Florine. The ability to pick up a Christian leader in Budapest and then transport him into Romania without intense border scrutiny and demeaning interrogation seemed bewildering to my new friend. But feeling I had to know the answer, from at least one person who lived during the revolution, I asked, "Did you ever think Romania would be free?"

The answer came quickly. "Not in a million years!" I queried further, "What about a month or two before when you started hearing reports of neighboring countries boldly throwing off the shackles of harsh regimes—did you think that maybe someday Romania would be free?"

Equally emphatic, the response came, "Absolutely not!"

"A week before?" I responded. "Surely the rumblings of freedom in neighboring nations gave hope."

"You just don't understand," Florine exclaimed. "The Securitaté (secret police) were everywhere and they were brutal."

Okay, I mused. Let me try once more: "Surely twenty-four hours before, when riots and resistance in Timisoara hit the news. Did you think then that Romania would someday be a free nation?"

Still with a tone that conveyed only hopelessness, his reply came, "Not even then, not even twenty-four hours before, we still did not anticipate it happening."

A spiritual and cultural transformation was simply unimaginable for those who had lived in darkness their entire lives. For those who had never experienced anything like it previously. Yet on Christmas Day, 1989, the brutal dictator Nicolae Ceausescu and his leadership were overthrown and a new nation was formed to the cheers and joyous celebration of the masses.

The sudden change in Romania brought more than the exchange of one political system for another. It was a massive revolution of the soul and spirit of a people.

But how did something so big and so impossible happen so quickly and so comprehensively?

GOD'S SUPERNATURAL INTERVENTION IS POSSIBLE IN ANY NATION!

It began with the way Scripture teaches that every heart, family, church, community, or nation is changed: *with an unusual season of repentance.* As the Romanian believers began to repent and cry out to God, extraordinary power was released in their lives. The little-told story of the revolution in Romania was that it was fueled by a revival in the Romanian church.[8]

That brief conversation with Florine was like a gift from heaven, stamped urgent and delivered by priority mail to the front door of my heart. I needed to hear it for my faith to be strengthened regarding God's ability to suddenly and supernaturally transform North America. If God could change a godless, atheistic, oppressed country like Romania in a moment, then God's supernatural intervention is possible in any nation!

I heard it often from one of my closest friends and founder of Life Action Ministries, Del Fehsenfeld Jr.: "As long as God is on His throne, revival is as possible as the sun rising tomorrow morning." In Romania, I saw that reality with my own eyes.

Holding On to God in Hope

I will never forget hearing about an exchange between two Christian leaders. They were leaving a meeting with the President in Washington, D.C. The meeting had been extended by nearly thirty minutes. The overwhelming moral and spiritual problems in America had been discussed.

Deeply discouraged as they were leaving the White House, one of the leaders turned to the other and said, "If we don't have revival, nothing else really matters." Wisely, the other leader replied, "And if we do have revival, nothing else really matters!"

There is no hope apart from revival. And there is no hope *like* revival!

Hope is the fuel that keeps on crying out to God for revival.

There are many hope-killers at work in our society today. And as things keep getting worse and worse around us, it is easy to despair that things will ever change.

Hope-killers believe that we are nearing the end of the ages. And since the Bible talks about the rise of wickedness before Christ's return, we should not expect things to get better. Though, historically, revival has always turned the tide of evil.[9]

Hope-killers think that wickedness has simply gone too far for mercy to prevail, and that judgment is the only option left.

So why in the face of all the headwinds against revival should we persevere in seeking God for it?

Yet Even Now

Let's return to our previous consideration of the prophet Joel's cry for God's leaders to weep between the porch and the altar—literally to weep for the people of God to come to the presence of God. It's noteworthy that Joel's name means "The Lord is God," reminding us that until we fully submit to God's authority, we won't experience His presence in revival.

Joel was fully aware that God's people in his day were far from God. The proof was visible to anyone who watched. Clearly he was in angst as he pled with the ministers of the Lord to weep and say, "Spare your people, O Lord, and make not your heritage a reproach, a byword among the nations. Why should they say among the peoples, 'Where is their God?'" (Joel 2:17 ESV).

That is the same question that we as believers find ourselves confronted with today. But after considering the moral, economic, political, and spiritual devastation that had ravaged and paralyzed Judah, Joel didn't miss God's remedy: "'Yet even now,' declares the Lord, 'return to me . . .'" (Joel 2:12 ESV).

Even now? Even after the loss of all their material blessings (1:17)? Even after the loss of their places of worship (1:9)? Even after the loss of joy and gladness (1:12, 16)? Economic prosperity was gone and emotional energy was depleted.

Yes, even in their darkest hour and most helpless moments, God still declared hope.

Hope. What an incredible word for us as God's people today! The call to this kind of hope is burning in my heart. It's a call (perhaps a final call) to fervently seek the Lord for wide-scale spiritual awakening. And it's a call not primarily to nations, but rather a fervent plea to God's people—*revival begins with us!*

The condition of our nation and world is ominous. We may,

in fact, be in the last days before the return of Christ. Though we don't know for certain, we do know that the indicators are more numerous than ever before. Five questions have helped to fuel my passion and focus the efforts of the OneCry call:

- *What if these really are the last days?* Many of God's people believe the end times are upon us. What if they are right and the time is short?

- *What if America is not an exception to the judgment of God?* Even though we have been blessed exceptionally by God as a nation, that does not make America an exception to God's ways. When we believe that somehow America will not reap the consequences of sin we have sown because of our extraordinary history, nothing could be further from the truth.

- *What if the promises of God for revival are still true today?* God promised the nation of Israel that humility, repentance, and prayer would lead to revival (2 Chronicles 7:14). And those same principles are repeated in the New Testament as timeless promises (see James 4:8 and Revelation 2–3).

- *What if there really is a "latter rain" in store for the earth as prophesied in the book of Joel?* This latter rain would be a sweeping move of the Holy Spirit resulting in a great harvest of souls prior to the second coming of Christ.

- *What if God is raising up a remnant of believers "for such a time as this"?* [I believe He is doing just that!]

Just as the prophet Joel anguished over the coldness, callousness, carnality, and complacency of God's people in his day, we, too, must possess this kind of intensity and urgency as we contemplate the need for revival in North America. We need the holy desperation that caused the prophet Jeremiah to cry out, "My eyes fail from weeping, I am in torment within; my heart is poured out on the ground because my people are destroyed" (Lamentations 2:11 NIV).

What about you? Do you sense the urgency in your own heart? Are you convinced that the time is now to cry out to God with fervency, passion, and perseverance? Do you want to be part of a great national, even worldwide, outpouring of the Spirit of God?

What if God is waiting for *your one cry*?

The Way Forward

In the second part of this book, my friend and colleague, Bill Elliff, will lay out six revival realities that can make OneCry a transformative reality in your life, family, church, community—and by God's grace for our nation and world! Then, in the final section, I'll share how you can join thousands of others who share a passion for spiritual awakening and who are seeking God together for personal, national, and global revival.

But before you read on, the words of the revivalist G. Campbell Morgan are instructive to all those who long for something more from God: "We cannot organize revival, but we can set our sails to catch the wind from heaven when God chooses to blow upon His people once again."[10]

Oh, that we might all be actively hoisting the sails, raising the anchors, and crying out for the wind of God's Spirit to blow across our land! Come, Lord Jesus! Do it again! Hear our cry! Hear our OneCry!

THINKING IT THROUGH

1. Can you recall one personal story of a time you found yourself crying out desperately for something? It can be an illustration from your personal life, your family, your business, a physical need, etc.

2. Many people, even unbelievers and atheists, tell stories of crying out to God in moments of great need. What is it that drives us to cry out to God in such times?

3. Does God really hear the urgent cries of people? Do you have an illustration of a time when God answered your desperate cry?

4. Do you agree that we are in a state of national spiritual emergency? Why or why not?

5. One of the goals of our study and prayer is to build our hope and faith that God can send nationwide revival. On a scale of 1-10 (10 being the most) how much faith do you have that what is happening in our nation—spiritually, morally, and culturally— can be changed? Mightily reversed? Is it even possible today?

6. What do you hope to gain out of this study?

CRYING OUT!

Spend a season in prayer around the following themes:

Thanksgiving:

- Give thanks for the POWER of God. Think of ways He has manifested His power to save a group of people in the past and in your own life. Give thanks to Him for His ability to do this whenever He desires.

- Give thanks to God for the thousands of people around the country who are thinking and praying about these things. Thank Him for those who are going through the OneCry Experience and pray that God would move in their lives and churches.

Intercession:

- Pray for God to develop your faith in His ability to send revival to the church and spiritual awakening to those who are unbelieving.

- Ask God to use these next eight weeks as a powerful tool in your life personally and with others who are studying these truths across the nation.

- Pray, at whatever level of faith you have, that God would send revival in our day!

Hear a heartfelt passionate cry for revival by
David Wilkerson and share your personal
cry at www.OneCryBook.com/part1.

PART TWO
SIX REVIVAL REALITIES

IT'S ABOUT HIM

*God hath had it much on his heart, from all eternity, to glorify
his dear and only-begotten Son; and there are some special
seasons that he appoints to that end, wherein he comes forth with
omnipotent power to fulfill his promise and oath to him. And
these times are times of remarkable pouring out of his Spirit, to
advance his kingdom; such a day is a day of his power . . . .*
Jonathan Edwards[1]

He was a king with a worldwide vision. Adolf Hitler rose to power after the first World War by promising the German people a return to their former glory. But his plans were far greater than simply the rise of the German nation. He longed for Germany to become the center of a new world order—a new kingdom.

He was so convinced of this outcome that plans were drawn for the redevelopment and renaming of Berlin into the capital of the world: "Germania." Hitler himself designed the central structure—The Great Hall—which would be the largest domed building in the world. Atop the dome was an eagle, but its claws did not hold the German swastika, but a globe, symbolizing Hitler's worldwide domination.

Many of the projects planned for the supposed "Germania" were scrapped as the war went on and funds became limited, but some of the structures remain today.

But it didn't go so well for this king. After a few years of unleashing hell upon Europe, his empire ended abruptly. Hitler did not end his reign on an exalted throne in a palace, but cowering in a concrete bunker where he took his own life on April 30, 1945. Today, his name is a byword for all that is evil and failed.

A Better King

But there was another King. As He entered human history, His plan was like no other: *He came to bring heaven to earth.*

This King's purpose was to open up eternity and let us experience the Divine. In one of His first public statements He announced that people should "repent, for the kingdom of heaven is at hand."[2] It had come. It was here. And He invited us to join Him.

In the ensuing days we began to see what that kingdom was like. Everywhere this humble King went, things changed. Blind people saw, lame people walked, the hungry were fed, the weak became strong. Simple fishermen became spiritual giants, tax collectors returned money they had extorted, and adulterers were lifted from the dust and transformed. People who had resigned themselves to a life of mindless insignificance or had been sidetracked by sin were swept into an exhilarating mission for which they had been fearfully and wonderfully made. It was intoxicating and miraculous because that is what heaven is like. That is what the *King* is like.

The Kingdom Manifesto

This King summarized His new kingdom with a manifesto: "You have heard it said . . . but I say" was the rhythm of His message. "You are familiar with the world's kingdom, but My kingdom is *very, very* different." The new norm was a supernatural people of unwavering truth but merciful grace. Of awesome holiness and stunning forgiveness. Of an internal change so profound that they could love anyone unconditionally—even their enemies. Because that is what heaven and those who dwell there are like. Pure, perfect, love. Heaven was coming down.

It was as if a stream of sunlight had broken through the clouds and poured itself out on mankind, washing people in the warmth of perfect affection and inviting them into its liberating light.

The Kingdom Entrance

He also announced the exclusivity of this kingdom. There was only one way to enter. You must see your spiritual need so greatly that you would gladly bow to this Sovereign. "Blessed are the poor in spirit,"[3] He said, who mourn over their detached and sinful condition and wholly surrender to the King in absolute meekness. These people have come to the end of themselves. By His grace, they have seen the disaster of a merely humanistic life and have cried out to the King, "Rule me!"

Those who cry out are saved and enter into the kingdom. The King has gladly chosen to give them the kingdom and sealed His pleasure with a promise: "Theirs is the kingdom of heaven."[4] They receive dual citizenship in the kingdom of this world and the kingdom of their God, and they can now operate in both simultaneously. In fact, their new assignment is to pray and serve fervently so that the Father's kingdom will come and His will be done "on earth as it is in heaven."[5]

They begin to live God-initiated lives, just like the King. When Jesus was on earth (operating as a man, but fully God), He showed us how we were to live. "I do nothing on My own initiative," He said, and "the things which I heard from [My Father] these I speak to the world."[6] His followers, empowered by His Spirit and instructed by His living Word, are able to peer into heaven, see what the Father instructs in any situation, and follow Him. As they do, heaven is brought to earth.

The Father's Intention

The Father, who sent His only begotten Son for this purpose, was adamant that only One could be King. After the Son's work on earth was accomplished, God "highly exalted him, and bestowed on him the name that is above every name, so that at the name of Jesus every knee should bow, in heaven and on earth and under the earth, and every tongue confess that Jesus Christ is Lord, to the glory of God the Father."[7]

THE GREATEST TRAGEDY OF THE CURRENT WORLD IS THAT WE FORGET ABOUT HIS KINGDOM.

Knowing and worshiping Him is the greatest privilege any human can experience. By giving Him dominion and control in our daily lives. By living a life of full surrender and joyous worship. A. W. Tozer said, "The reason why many are still troubled, still seeking, still making little forward progress is because they haven't yet come to the end of themselves. We're still trying to give orders, and interfering with God's work within us."[8]

By the King's gracious intervention, He is now adored and worshiped by millions. But the greatest tragedy of the current world is that we forget about His kingdom and fail to bow before the King. Enamored by the dazzling allurements around us and the offerings of our Enemy, even His followers are often pulled away from "the simplicity and purity of devotion to [Jesus] Christ."[9]

The Dark Night of an Ignored King

God's kingdom has a devious and powerful enemy. One who is determined to destroy God and everything related to Him, and he is relentless in his attack. His stated purpose is to steal, kill, and destroy[10] and he's good at his craft.

The garden of Eden records the tragic story of his first assault on mankind and the turn of Adam and Eve from God's rule. When that occurred, death came. The rest of human history is a continual battle between good and evil. The Bible records this in bold relief as we see individuals and nations turning away from God, the ensuing judgment from the King, the desperate cry of the repentant, and God's sovereign intervention in revival among His people and spiritual awakening among the lost.

We see this pattern not only on an individual level, but also on a corporate or national level. If it were not for the gracious work of God's judgments that brings us to desperation—His convicting hand that leads to His converting hand—we would never turn to Him.

Cycle of Spiritual Awakening

Worship and Mission

Awakening among Unbelievers

Decline

Revival among Believers

Discipline / Judgment

Crying Out

The Critical Role of Spiritual Awakenings

This cycle of spiritual awakening is vital to our spiritual survival and God's purposes. In times of deep, national decay, it seems that the only element that can bring the comprehensive course correction needed is a widespread movement of revival and awakening. When we cry out, He revives His church in dramatic measure and then—for a season—sends an outpouring of spiritual awakening to the lost in rapid fire. At such times, hundreds, thousands, even millions of people are converted. His endgame is to quickly bring to life those who are "dead in their trespasses and sins" so that they would honor the Son. In heaven, the Lamb of God is worshiped constantly.

> **REALITY #1**
> **IT'S ABOUT HIM:** *A spiritual awakening is the visible invasion of the King and His kingdom.*

Spiritual awakening advances His kingdom on earth, and that which is done above is done below. The King is enthroned to His rightful place in thousands of human hearts, and the revived and expanded church worships Him.

Our Recent Past

In the first 150 years of American history, God sent such awakenings every thirty to sixty years: the First Great Awakening (1730–1740), the Second Great Awakening (1790–1830), the Prayer Revival of 1857–1858, and the Welsh Revival of 1904–1906, which expanded during the next few years to impact the US and many countries around the world. All served to provide dramatic course corrections, bringing Christ front and center to our consciousness and worship.

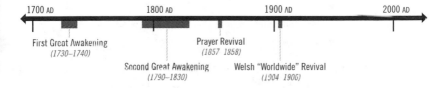

1700 AD · 1800 AD · 1900 AD · 2000 AD

First Great Awakening
(1730–1740)

Second Great Awakening
(1790–1830)

Prayer Revival
(1857 1858)

Welsh "Worldwide" Revival
(1904 1906)

Jonathan Edwards, perhaps our greatest American theologian and a firsthand witness of the First Great Awakening, reminded us of how quickly God can turn a society back to honor the Son. He said that in seasons of awakening . . .

> *the work of God is carried on with greater speed and swiftness, and there are often instances of sudden conversions at such a time. So it was in the apostles' days, when there was a time of the most extraordinary pouring out of the Spirit. . . . How quick and sudden were conversions in those days . . . so it is in some degree whenever there is an extraordinary pouring out of the Spirit of God. . . .*[11]

Samuel Davies, who was known as the apostle of Virginia and became the president of Princeton University, recounted the following in 1747:

> *About sixteen years ago, in the northern colonies, when all religious concern was much out of fashion, and the people generally lay in a dead sleep in sin, having at best but the form of godliness, but nothing of the power; when the country was in peace and prosperity, free from the calamities of war, and epidemical sickness; when, in short, there were no extraordinary calls to repentance; suddenly a deep, general concern about eternal things spread through the country; sinners started out from their slumbers, broke off from their vices, began to cry out, what shall we do to be saved? And made it the great business of their life to prepare for the world to come.*
>
> *Then the gospel seemed almighty, and carried all before it. It pierced the very hearts of men with an irresistible power. I have*

seen thousands at once melted down under it; all eager to hear as for life, and hardly a dry eye to be seen among them. . . .[12]

A genuine, national movement of spiritual awakening produces astounding results. J. Edwin Orr (one of our greatest American revival historians) recounted that in the First Great Awakening, 50,000 came to Christ in New England out a population of 340,000 (almost 15 percent).

During the Second Great Awakening, conservative estimates record that the Methodist denomination grew by 1400 percent while the American population was growing at only 200 percent. In three counties in Virginia over a three-month span, 3200 people were converted.[13]

During the Prayer Revival of 1857–1858, there were a reported 50,000 coming to Christ weekly. The Holy Trinity Church in Chicago had 157 members in 1857 (before the awakening) and 1400 members in 1858. In New York City alone, during the height of the movement, 10,000 people were coming to Christ every single week. Out of a population of 30 million Americans, one million came to faith in Christ.[14]

In the Welsh Revival, 100,000 people were gloriously converted in nine months!

And the results were lasting. People wondered if the Welsh Revival was real or just an emotional phenomenon. J. Edwin Orr reminds us that "five years later, Dr. J. V. Morgan wrote a book to debunk the (Welsh) revival, his main criticism being that, of 100,000 joining the churches in five months of excitement, after five years only 80,000 still stood in the membership of those churches!"[15]

We now have an estimated population of nearly 320 million in America. If God were to manifest Himself in the same way as He did in the 1857–1858 revival, we would see over 10 million people come to Christ in two years. This would be 95,000 new believers every week over twenty-four months!

Awakenings Radically Change Culture

Samuel Davies reminded us from the vantage point of the Second Great Awakening that "there are eras when only a large outpouring of the Spirit can produce a public general reformation."[16] He witnessed firsthand how revival and awakening brought a cultural change that nothing else could accomplish.

The pastor of Saint John's–Wood Presbyterian Church declared after the Welsh Revival, in which 100,000 people came to Christ in nine months in 1904–1905, that "the mighty unseen breath of the Spirit was doing in a month more than centuries of legislation could accomplish."[17]

No political equation can resolve the deepest problems we face as a nation. Look at three of our greatest spiritual and social diseases: abortion, divorce, and pornography.

We are so calloused about abortion that it hardly registers with us anymore that we are killing over one million babies a year. I once visited the Incan ruins at Chichen Itza in Mexico with my wife. We were awed by the massive pyramids and amazing structures, wondering what kind of civilized people were able to accomplish such feats. Then our guide took us to a large pit and showed us where the babies were sacrificed. Suddenly, our stomachs turned as we were reminded that any nation that could slaughter its young was no civilized country.

We are all sick of the horror of divorce. No one wins. Children are devastated, husbands and wives are crushed, and succeeding generations are demoralized and find themselves afraid to enter into marriage because their own parents didn't succeed. Sadly, the divorce rate in the church in America is only slightly different than among unbelievers. Every pastor is brokenhearted about the decimation that is coming as a result of broken homes and broken lives. We have more marriage teaching and training than any time in human history and yet it seems to have little effect.

And pornography. Three million dollars are spent every second on Internet pornography. Every thirty-nine seconds a new Internet pornography site is created in America. Tragically, America leads the world with 89 percent of the pornographic web pages worldwide (over 244 million pages). The next closest competitor is Germany with ten million pages.[18] There is no greater plague in our land as it destroys men, women (one of every three viewers is female), and children at unprecedented levels. It is epidemic and killing the home, the church, and the nation.

> **WE NEED A MASSIVE COURSE CORRECTION THAT ONLY A SOVEREIGN KING CAN BRING.**

Pastors and churches are seeking valiantly to hold back the flood of abortion, divorce, and pornography with little to show for it. We throw up our hands in resignation, realizing that the best efforts of our churches are making little progress.

What could possibly stop this tsunami of moral ills? Is there any conceivable solution?

Only a mighty spiritual awakening as we have known in our past can reverse these plagues! We need a massive course correction that only a Sovereign King can bring. Without it we will continue to spiral down into moral oblivion. We need God to "rend the heavens and come down"[19] in manifest, saving power. And He has done it before. Every major awakening in American history has been followed by extensive cultural transformation that nothing else could accomplish. During the Welsh Revival, the jails were emptied, drunkenness was cut in half as were unwed pregnancies, and the judges were issued white gloves signifying there were no more cases to try!

When God opens heaven and releases a rapid expansion of His kingdom on earth, everything changes. These Divine invasions that we call "spiritual awakenings" are beyond-the-norm, over-the-top, clearly recognizable interventions by a gracious God, that are easily distinguishable from the regular work of the Church. During great, widespread awakenings, the doors of heaven are opened with extraordinary wideness, and we see and experience His kingdom coming to earth. A reminder of the unfathomable love of God.

What is tragic is that most of us have no context for these seasons of awakening. We've read the biblical accounts and perhaps some stories from church history, but we have not seen with our own eyes moments of mighty, nationwide, spiritual awakening. We have no fathers or grand fathers that have passed firsthand accounts into our soul. Because of this, our faith is weak and our prayers are small. We find it hard to conceive or believe that God could send us such times of nationwide outpouring.

But our lack of experience doesn't negate their reality or God's power to do it again!

A Story of Hope

In the fall of 2010, at the church where I pastor, we sensed a growing desperation for revival. We called our people to forty days of prayer and fasting. In January, we began to meet on the first Monday of each month to cry out for revival. There seemed to be a growing sense of expectancy.

In April of 2011, a wonderful mercy-drop of revival and awakening occurred in the church. While preaching on the quenching of the Holy Spirit, the Lord stopped me in the middle of my message and told me I was done. After a brief bit of argument with Him, I told the congregation that it was time for me to stop.

Immediately a former missionary stood up in the congregation and pled with us to obey Christ "right now" and quench the Spirit no longer. The altar filled, people began to come to the microphone, and the service, which normally ended at 12:30 p.m., lasted until 3:00 p.m. An Air Force pilot came to the microphone to confess that God had been prompting his heart to be baptized for four years and he had ignored Him. "I wonder what damage I have done to this church by not following Christ and quenching His Spirit." He asked if he could be baptized right then and began to take off his shoes in preparation! Before the service closed, four more people had surrendered to Christ and followed Him in baptism.

The next night we were scheduled to have an evening of prayer, which we had been doing on the first Monday of each month. Instead of the seventy-plus that had been attending, the auditorium was filled with people, and that service lasted three hours with more people coming to Christ. Testimonies were given, people were saved and baptized, money was spontaneously given to meet needs, prayer was powerful, and lives were transformed. We decided to meet the next night, taking it one day at a time and, to our amazement, that spontaneous revival lasted *five consecutive weeks*, every night except Saturday.

Every single day, to the best of our knowledge, people were coming to Christ and gladly confessing their faith. Our people were sharing Christ with everyone they met. Sixty-five people were baptized. Cars and rings were given. Money was flowing at such a rate between people that there seemed to be no more needy among us, just as seen in Acts 4. One man who was a forty-year alcoholic was dramatically delivered (and is sober to this day). I stood up one night and read Acts 2 and remarked through tears that it was the first time I could honestly say that everything that was happening in the early church was happening, in some measure, in our church. It was a continuous prayer meeting and God's presence was amazingly clear among His people. Many people began to hear of these mercy-drops and came from all over the country to join with us.

We did not advertise. We did not promote. We could have never orchestrated such a movement. It was simply an intervention of God to bring revival to His church and spiritual awakening to the lost.

I have wondered why God chose to bring this wonderful season of refreshing and salvation to our church. And I have concluded that its purpose for us was to build our faith. To give us context for our prayers. To take us deeper to understand what God can accomplish in an instant when He chooses to manifest Himself.

We have six hundred churches in Central Arkansas where I pastor, an area of roughly 500,000 people. If the same measure of God's mercy descended upon our city that occurred in our church, we would see 39,000 people saved in five weeks! What would this infusion of that number of genuine, new believers do to our schools? Our communities and businesses? Our government?

I would not believe this could be possible except for the fact that I have studied the history of spiritual awakening. I understand something of the power of God, and I have seen firsthand what even a small measure of His manifest presence can accomplish. He has done this in this way and greater in the past . . . and He is the same "yesterday, today, and forever."

What would occur in your city if 10 percent of the population were suddenly awakened to their deep spiritual poverty in a way that brought them to genuine repentance and complete submission to the rule of the King? His kingdom would come in greater measure and the Son would be adored.

Good Kings Are Always Loved

Good kings are always loved by their followers and feared by their adversaries. And King Jesus is the ultimate monarch. When God has chosen in human history to bring His kingdom down in revival and spiritual awakening, Jesus is adored. God's true church— recently revived and dramatically expanded—rises up in glorious worship and moves forward in glad obedience. God's intent to honor His Son is brilliantly realized.

The central hymn of the Welsh Revival was not about the phenomena that were occurring, but about the love of Christ. It was a song of humble gratitude for the cross and its effects, and a prayer of kingdom consecration. It is the kind of song that erupts from the earth when the kingdom of heaven comes and the King is ruling in human hearts. Read it slowly and you will hear the echoes of heaven's song.

HERE IS LOVE

Here is love, vast as the ocean,
Lovingkindness as the flood,
When the Prince of Life, our Ransom,
Shed for us His precious blood.
Who His love will not remember?
Who can cease to sing His praise?
He can never be forgotten,
Throughout Heaven's eternal days.

On the mount of crucifixion,
Fountains opened deep and wide;
Through the floodgates of God's mercy
Flowed a vast and gracious tide.
Grace and love, like mighty rivers,
Poured incessant from above,
Heaven's peace and perfect justice
Kissed a guilty world in love.

Let me all Thy love accepting,
Love Thee, ever all my days;
Let me seek Thy kingdom only
And my life be to Thy praise,
Thou alone shall be my glory,
Nothing in the world I see.
Thou hast cleansed and sanctified me,
Thou Thyself hast set me free.

In Thy truth Thou dost direct me
By Thy Spirit through Thy Word;
And Thy grace my need is meeting,
As I trust in Thee, my Lord.
Of Thy fullness Thou art pouring

Thy great love and power on me,
Without measure, full and boundless,
Drawing out my heart to Thee.[20]

We must pursue spiritual awakening for the right reason. We groan under the oppression of the world, the flesh, and the devil. We long for relief, and we should. But we should cry out earnestly for a sweeping awakening for God's glory. We should pray that God would intervene in our nation so that we would no longer deprive His Son, Jesus Christ, of His rightful place in every dimension of His world and every corner of our hearts. He deserves our full adoration and joyful obedience.

Awakenings, seen in the purest light, are about Him, and it is time to cry out for a fresh, Christ-honoring movement now.

THINKING IT THROUGH

1. Look again at the Cycle of Spiritual Awakening diagram on page 51. Where do you think the church in America is on this cycle? What evidences illustrate this?

2. How would you define real, authentic revival? (It's important to know what we should be praying for!)

3. What do you think it would look and feel like if God sent a city-wide or nationwide revival and season of spiritual awakening? Be as specific as you can.

4. What might change in your city if 10 percent of the entire population came to authentic faith in Christ in the next twelve months?

5. Do think it's possible for God to send such an awakening to your city and to America? Why or why not?

6. What do you think God's main purpose is in revival? Why would He ever bless us with such a mighty outpouring of His Spirit?

CRYING OUT!

Spend a season in prayer around the following themes:

Thanksgiving:
- Thank God for His kingdom and His ability to bring His kingdom down to earth. Name specific aspects of this kingdom that you desire for God to bring to our nation.

- Thank Him for what He has done in the past.

- Thank Him for His ability to send revival.

Intercession:
- Ask Him to increase your faith and the faith of the believers in the churches in your city.

- Pray for as many churches in your city as you can by name.

REVIEW—Revival Realities:

1. **It's About Him:** *A spiritual awakening is the visible invasion of the King and His kingdom.*

Watch the accompanying video to Reality 1, print the Cycle of Spiritual Awakening, and watch a video on how Great Awakenings radically change culture— all at www.OneCryBook.com/reality1.

IT STARTS HERE

*A man by his sin may waste himself, which is
to waste that which on earth is most like God. This
is man's greatest tragedy and God's heaviest grief.*
A. W. Tozer[1]

It was one o'clock in the morning when the Lord awakened a young man from his sleep, prompting him to rise from his bed and do business with God. Instead of the normal response of a young student, this twenty-six-year-old chose to heed God's call. For the next three hours, God opened up the Scriptures and taught His eager disciple fresh truths from His Word.

The next night the same drill occurred. And the next. Night after night, for many months, God poured His life and truth into a willing heart. This amazing season of personal, Word-saturated illumination and revival was so sacred that the young man would barely talk about it later. The culmination of those early morning hours was a God-given vision to see his tiny nation come to Christ through a revival among God's people and spiritual awakening among the lost. In fact, he began to pray that 100,000 people would be converted.

Soon the young learner was ready and he felt prompted to return to his hometown and share with his church four simple, but profound challenges. His pastor allowed him a few minutes after a Monday night service where he called the people to confess all known sin, put away any doubtful habits, obey the Spirit promptly, and confess Christ publicly.

What happened next confirmed that it could not have been the mere persuasiveness of the young student that moved people to respond. People came back the next night, and the next, and the next, and soon the crowds exploded. God flooded that church with His presence, and then another church, and another until the whole nation of Wales was ablaze with God's glory in a matter of weeks. Each night almost every church in every village was filled. There were no planned programs but the simple movement of God's Spirit, breaking His people and then calling the lost to Himself. And in the next nine months, 100,000 people came to faith in Christ in Wales.

Before the awakening, God was working across Wales in many individual lives and churches, bringing believers to fresh surrender. But students of the Welsh Revival of 1904–1905 would later trace the national ignition point to the personal revival that Evan Roberts experienced, and the meetings in Moriah Chapel in Loughor in September 1904.

It starts with one.

The Nature of Reviving

> REALITY #2
> **IT STARTS HERE:** *National awakenings begin with personal reviving.*

When we hear that a theatrical play has been "revived," we know that something that happened in the past has returned. It's brought to life again. A spiritual revival occurs when God brings His people back to life. "Awakening" is a term that refers to what God does to unbelievers, supernaturally waking them from the dead to new life. But "revival" is a fresh surrender among God's own children. It is the "extraordinary movement of God, *in the hearts of His people*, that produces extraordinary spiritual results."[2]

You cannot *"re"*vive something that has not been "vived"! When God moves in revival, He intervenes by His power to bring His children and churches to renewed life again. God can do whatever He desires in whatever way He desires. And so, we cannot insist that He is bound to this progression (revival *first* among His children, then spiritual awakening among the lost). But experientially that is usually the progression in great, nationwide movements.

God longs to revive His people. And it starts with you.

Missing What Matters

My oldest grandson, Parker, played his first baseball game at the age of four. It was like a national holiday as the whole family, aunts and uncles and grandparents, all arrived to see the inaugural performance of the next Babe Ruth.

He looked the part from the top of his little baseball cap all the way down to his little baseball cleats. Ready for action. His dad had coached him well, reminding him to put his hands on his knees in a crouching position to be ready to move in either direction. They worked on the "crouch" a lot and Parker had it down.

The problem was, that was all he got. When the ball was hit, he didn't move an inch—his eyes fixated on the plate, hands still on his knees. At first, we thought it was an aberration, a temporary oversight, a brief mental lapse, or maybe a revolutionary new technique. But inning after inning confirmed our suspicions, particularly as the ball (to which he was absolutely oblivious) almost hit him in the head as he remained in his crouched position. Parker was a Hall of Fame Croucher, but not much of a baseball player!

It's possible to do some things really well, but miss the main thing. To crouch but never really get in the game. Wouldn't it be tragic to come to the end of your life and realize you had missed what mattered most? That you had invested your time and energy in all kinds of activity, but never looked up and discovered the primary objective of life?

> **WOULDN'T IT BE TRAGIC TO COME TO THE END OF YOUR LIFE AND REALIZE YOU HAD MISSED WHAT MATTERED MOST?**

The Main Thing

A man once asked Jesus Christ what the most important commandment was in His new kingdom. Jesus didn't hesitate in His answer.

"You shall love the Lord your God with all your heart, and with all your soul, and with all your mind." This is the great and foremost commandment.[3]

God's intent in building His kingdom is to gather a people who will know Him and love Him, just as He first loved us. It is more a family than an organization. He is so committed to this that He made us in His image, giving us the ability to choose to love Him (enabled, of course, by His grace). In this way, love would be a real affection, not the mindless movement of an android.

But with that ability we can also choose other gods to love.

Falling Out of Love Is Possible

The believers at Ephesus were commended for their sound doctrine, for refusing to tolerate false teachers, and for perseverance combined with good works. They were crouching well. Jesus commended them for their faithfulness.

I know your deeds and your toil and perseverance, and that you cannot tolerate evil men, and you put to the test those who call themselves apostles, and they are not, and you found them to be false; and you have perseverance and have endured for My name's sake, and have not grown weary.[4]

But then Christ leveled the worst possible comment any true follower of Christ could hear.

But I have this against you, that you have left your first love.[5]

"You don't love Me anymore," Jesus said in effect. "You have a few of the basic forms correct, but you've lost the heart of it all. You're missing the main thing. And without that, nothing else really matters."

Imagine a wife welcoming her husband home one day with these words: "Honey, I'm glad you're home. By the way, I just wanted you to know that I plan to cook and clean our home. I'll make sure it's a great environment. I'll help raise our kids and get them off to school each day. I know those things are my duty and I'm going to fulfill them. But there's one thing that I need you to know—I just don't love you anymore."

Devastating!

The relationship between a bride and groom is built upon love. Passionate affection is the fuel for every great marriage, and without it the home disintegrates.

And, as you probably know, our earthly marriages are intended by God to merely be a picture of the greater union of Christ and His bride, the church.

Imagine a Christian, saved by God's grace, saying to the Groom, Jesus Christ, "I want You to know that I'll come to church most Sundays. I'll occasionally read my Bible because I know I should. I'll give a little bit, support missions, and maybe even teach children in Bible study. I'm committed to doing most of the Christian stuff. But, I just want You to know—I don't really love You anymore."

Our Groom's greatest desire is not His bride's activity, but her undivided affection. Christ doesn't want mere form, but passion. He longs for YOU. He wants an intimate relationship. In fact, He died for that intimacy to occur. He knows that all the right works flow from a passionate heart. But without love, a marriage—earthly or heavenly—is doomed. Love provides things that are found nowhere else.

Love for Christ is **empowering**. You can operate only so long out of duty, and not very well. Love fuels you with the passion for a sustaining relationship.

And love is **intriguing**. When you love someone, you want to know more about them, and you discover that a lifetime cannot reveal all the inner reaches of their heart. When we are in love with Jesus we are drawn in, captured by the height and depth and breadth of His love. Our great desire is to know Him and experience Him in ever-increasing intimacy.

True love is more **fulfilling** than anything else as Christ becomes our greatest longing and greatest satisfaction. When we are experiencing the love of Christ, there is no need to look for joy anywhere else.

Ecstasy and delight are essential to the believer's soul . . . we are not meant to live without spiritual exhilaration . . . The believer is in spiritual danger if he allows himself to go for any length of time without tasting the love of Christ. When Christ ceases to fill the heart with satisfaction, our souls will go in silent search of other lovers.[6]

And love for Christ is **contagious**. Mere religious duty is not only insanely boring to us, but incredibly unappetizing to all who observe our dutiful rituals. Look at the next generation and see how nauseated they are by merely formal Christianity. Their church attendance after age eighteen tells you what they think of passionless religion.

But when you are around a believer who is deeply in love with Jesus, the aroma fills the room and calls you to join them. Our love for Christ is our most obvious witness.

It's possible to wake up and realize that you simply don't love Christ anymore. And, if you don't, you've missed what matters most.

Revival begins with brutally honest evaluation. No excuses, no blaming of others, just accepting full responsibility for where you really are. What is your answer right now if Jesus were to stand before you and ask, *"Do you love Me?"*

It's Fixable

Jesus would not have come to the Ephesian church to warn them and call them back if there was not a way to fall in love all over again. It's possible by His grace and your aggressive cooperation with Him. He gave us very simple, doable instructions. Personal revival begins here for every true follower of Jesus.

REMEMBER

Remember from where you have fallen . . . .[7]

The best way to gauge slippage is to look back to where you started in your walk with Christ. To remember. To compare the past with the present. Remembering, though, takes time and intentional thought. Here are a few questions to jog your memory. It might be wise to take an afternoon alone with Him to fully and truthfully deal with these questions. Take a notebook and write out your answers.

- Do you remember when you first came to Christ? What was your love for Him like in those days?

- Is there anything that you were once willing to do for Christ that you are unwilling to do now? If yes, what and why?

- Think back over the three greatest highlights of your spiritual journey. Was there a greater passion then than there is now? Why?

- Have you lost your extravagance in love? Has your relationship with Him become mundane and routine?

- As you look back, where did you begin to lose your fervency for Christ?

- Jesus said you are to love the Lord with "**all** your heart, and with **all** your soul, and with **all** your mind."[8] Does He dominate **all** your affections? Are there closets of your heart, your soul, your mind that are off limits to Him? That are preoccupied with other things?

- What do you love more than Jesus? What takes precedence over time with Him?

- What would you be willing to give to return to the days of your greatest passion for Christ?

It is not enough to *remember* and then wallow in the despair of lost love. The Lord gains nothing by merely making you feel guilty for your loss. It is the indispensable first step, but He calls you to more in the process of personal revival.

REPENT

Remember from where you have fallen, and repent . . . [9]

Not long ago I was asked to do a wedding out of town and my wife joined me. They placed us in a wonderful room in an old, romantic hotel. After the rehearsal, we had the evening to ourselves. We walked along the boulevard and talked the night away. We have eight children, so a night like this is a rarity and a treasure.

During those hours, I remembered how much I loved this woman with whom I had spent two-thirds of my life. I remembered that I'd rather be with her than anyone on the face of the earth. It had been awhile since I had just looked into her face like that and it was thrilling. I fell in love all over again.

The next day we were driving home from the wedding and my heart was overwhelmed with my love for her. And sometimes, there's nothing more intimate than holding your wife's hand. Without a word, I slipped my hand into hers . . . *with all my heart.*

Repentance is a deep, Spirit-wrought change of mind that produces a change of direction. It is coming to realize what you've lost and what you need. It is seeing the value once again of simple, pure devotion to Jesus Christ. It is taking your eyes off silly, valueless gods and peering again into the face of Christ. It's falling in love again.

If we need to repent, it is because we have turned. Once, our gaze was fixed on the face of Christ. We looked to Him, loved Him, and would do anything for Him. But somewhere along the way, something else captured our attention. It could be the material things of this world, or the love of comfort and pleasure, or the pursuit of prestige and reputation—the lust to have everyone like us. When our eyes shift, our direction changes. (Just try to teach your teenager to drive and see if this is not true!) Often, before we even realize what has happened, the world has captured our attention and we have turned our backs toward Christ.

That is why *remembering*, looking back, is so important. When we remember from where we've fallen and the marvelous joy of intimacy with Christ, we are willing to repent. Real repentance is not driven as much by what we turn *from* as what we turn *to*. We long to come home, and then we begin to turn in that direction by the grace of God.

Sometimes repentance happens in a moment. But for most of us, going home is a process. It can be sped along by spending concentrated, intentional time with Him. We may need to go on a retreat with the Groom. To get away and let Him talk to us and hold us in His arms. We need to take deliberate time to listen to what He is saying through His precious Word. Maybe we need to sit with an open notebook and ask God to show us every false god that has garnered our attention and every sin that has flowed from that idol worship. Perhaps we need to fast to quiet the noise of other gods and humble our soul through this invaluable, forgotten exercise, so we can hear the whispers of the Lover of our soul. Whatever it takes, we must pay the price to make the turn home to His heart. (See Appendix 3 for a "Personal Revival Checklist.")

Isn't it time for you to repent? Why would you turn your back on the One who loves you with a steadfast love? The only One who can satisfy you? The One who is waiting for you even now?

Wouldn't you like to slip your hand in His again . . . *with all your heart?*

RETURN

Remember from where you have fallen, and repent
and do the deeds you did at first . . . .[10]

When we are cooperating with God in His gracious work of personal revival, we return to Him. And with that return, good works begin to flow from our relationship. What kind of deeds? The joyful actions of crazy, reckless, extravagant love!

Remember the first time you fell in love with someone? The long phone calls? The homemade cards? The gift you bought that you couldn't afford? The big banner you made for the one you loved? Real love erupts.

There is no prescription for this in our spiritual walk because different people express their love in different ways. Some people are loud shouters, some humble pray-ers. Some sing at the top of their lungs while others show their love by quiet, relentless acts of service. All of these activities are vain and worthless if they are done from a loveless heart. But when we are consumed with Christ, they become vibrant expressions of our passion.

But there are some deeds that are universal when we fall head-over-heels in love with Christ. The following are some of the signs of a revived heart.

Time

When you love Christ you don't ignore Him. You want to spend time with Him daily. When He wakes you up earlier than you thought you needed in the morning, or keeps you up all night, you remember that He is wanting to speak to you, love you, and equip you, and you joyfully give Him the precious gift of time. You love to worship Him with others, and time is not a consideration. And each and every day, the whole day is His.

Talk

Revived people commune with the One they love. They talk and listen intently with Him through the Word and prayer. The greatest moments of revival in my life have been the sweetest, most consistent times of uninterrupted communion with Jesus. You learn what it means to "pray without ceasing"[11] because you can't stand to be away from Him and you see the value of His leadership and input on every decision. There are even moments when you just love to sit in His presence and tell Him you love Him. You love to talk with Him privately and in a group with others. A revived believer prays.

Testimony

People who are in love are almost obnoxious as they talk about their beloved. The greatest reason most believers don't share Christ with others is that they have nothing to say. It has been a long time since they had a life-changing encounter with Christ. There is no desire (only a dull sense of duty) to witness to others or give testimony of God's goodness or deliverance.

But when you are revived, you cannot help but speak about what [you've] seen and heard.[12] You are unashamed of Him. In humility you don't think less of yourself, you just think of yourself less and you talk of Him more. You can talk to a total stranger or your best friend as "the mouth speaks out of that which fills the heart."[13]

When your heart is *filled* with Him, your mouth will *speak* of Him.

Treasures

When you see Christ afresh, you remember that every single thing you have—indeed, every breath—is a gift from a gracious Father. You find yourself surrendering everything back into His control. When He tells you to fill up someone's car with gas, or pay for someone's meal, you do it gladly.

When the offering moment comes in the assembly of His children, you give generously. You are not concerned with how little you can give to ease your conscience, but how much you can give and bless God by helping others. You become like the One you're gazing at, for He is the ultimate giver.

You are moved by the needs of others because Christ's compassion is constraining you and you long for them to know His blessing and salvation. And you quickly respond. Selfishness is superseded by love-driven generosity.

Our deeds are an evidence of where we are spiritually. Wouldn't it make sense that revived people, those who are passionately in love with Jesus, are generously different?

Turn Out the Lights

As a pastor for over forty years, I've dealt with a lot of parents who have prodigal children. Nothing is more gut-wrenching to a mom or dad than a child who turns their back on God and on their family and walks away . . . usually down very destructive paths. But the worst pain is the lost love and strained relationship.

Does Christ feel this when we lose our love for Him? Is He grieved when we engage in petty, fruitless things that will ultimately destroy us and others (even if these things look respectable)? If He loves us perfectly, is He burdened when we squander our love on the gods of this world?

Our ability to choose is a wonderful provision from our Creator. But it can be deadly when used to choose other gods. And no one knows this more than the King. In fact, He put a sobering "PS" on the letter to the Ephesians to drive home the consequences of a loveless life.

> *Therefore remember from where you have fallen, and repent and do the deeds you did at first;* ***or else I am coming to you and will remove your lampstand out of its place—unless you repent.*** [14]

Jesus is determined to glorify His Father. And when His family is not representing the Father well, He knows it will ultimately lead to a poor picture of God. Our task in life is to give the world a right opinion of God. An unrevived church or believer is a hollow, life-less caricature of true Christianity. And Jesus will not let that go on indefinitely . . . for our sake, for the world's sake, and for His sake.

Jesus warned the Ephesians believers. If they did not return, He would be forced to remove their lampstand from its place. He indicated that He would attend to this Himself. The church would lose its power and ultimately its existence. And He has not changed in His judgments.

We would think this is impossible, but we have all seen the growing darkness of dying churches. Once vibrant, full of love for Christ, and shedding light in every direction, many churches have slowly turned from their love of Jesus. They've grown affectionate toward their comfort, prestige, programs, buildings, maybe even the fellowship that the church affords. But they don't deeply love Christ. The car is there, but the engine is gone. And an engineless car is going nowhere. "There is nothing more useless than a merely formal Christian," said Martyn Lloyd–Jones.[13]

A church or a believer who fails to repent and return is doomed to a fruitless, faithless, formal life. Spiritual sterility prevails and they bear no spiritual children. They may go through the motions of Christianity, but the light is gone and God is grieved. They could have had so much and done so much, but they simply missed so much.

Why Not Now?

Churches are composed of individual believers (like you) who make the choice to remember, repent, and return, or not. If you long for national awakening where millions are ushered into the kingdom, it begins with your return to your first love. And loving Him—fully and extravagantly—fills the world with the irresistible fragrance of love.

MARY'S LOVE

She sensed the subtle sadness of His eyes,
She felt it coming soon, His time was near.
What humble act that He would not despise
Would comfort and subdue His hidden tears?

She took the costly fragrance of her love,
And gave the all she had with sudden whim,
Anointing her Messiah from above,
She knelt before the Lord and worshipped Him!

And then, with not a thought of public shame,
She loosed the band that held her silken hair,
And out of adoration for this Name,

She ministered to Him with gentle care.

And suddenly the supper room was filled,
With fragrances of love unusually sweet.
The picture of this precious love had stilled
The others as they watched her at His feet.

What matchless love the Master can evoke;
What ardor doth spring forth from hearts He's touched.
And though we were not there the night He spoke,
O, Jesus, may we love you ere that much![16]

THINKING IT THROUGH

1. Do you think your individual spiritual life affects whether or not we see God's presence and power in your church, city, and nation? Why or why not?

2. What are some of the gods or idols that most of us turn to other than Christ?

3. On a scale of 1 to 10 (10 being the most fervent love and surrender to Christ), where would you say your spiritual life is now and why?

4. What do you think must happen for a believer to return to his/her first love? To fall passionately in love with Christ all over again?

5. What would a believer who is living in fresh, personal revival look like? How would it affect his/her family? Church? Community?

6. What is the next step for you to experience personal revival?

7. What do you think will happen to your life and your church if you and others you know choose not to repent and return?

CRYING OUT!

Spend an extended season in prayer around the following themes:

Thanksgiving:

- Thank God for your salvation and for the cross. If you have never surrendered to Christ and received His forgiveness, take time in prayer to do that now, repenting of your sin and crying out to Him for forgiveness.

- Thank God for His forgiveness and love . . . for His grace and mercy that makes salvation and personal revival possible.

Intercession:

- Quietly and deliberately walk through the list of questions previously listed on page 72.

- Spend time repenting and crying out to God for His cleansing and mercy.

- Read and pray through Psalm 51.

- Work through the "Personal Revival Checklist" in Appendix 3.

REVIEW—Revival Realities:

1. It's About Him: *A spiritual awakening is the visible invasion of the King and His kingdom.*
2. **It Starts Here:** *National awakenings begin with personal reviving.*

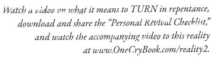

Watch a video on what it means to TURN in repentance,
download and share the "Personal Revival Checklist,"
and watch the accompanying video to this reality
at www.OneCryBook.com/reality2.

THE PAIN WE NEED

*Indeed I tremble for my country when I reflect that
God is just; that his justice cannot sleep forever.*
Thomas Jefferson
(Inscribed on the Jefferson Memorial in Washington, D.C.)

I was a carefree kid, running through a construction site. I should have known better as I hopped over piles of nail-embedded lumber in my Converse All Star tennis shoes. In my youth, those shoes had no padding and little support. So I felt it when a rusty nail went shooting up through the sole of my shoe and planted itself in the arch of my foot. It hurts me right now just to write about it!

Excruciating pain coursed through my body. I pulled the nail out and ran home where my mother took me immediately to the emergency room to get a tetanus shot. Wise, as usual. Because an unattended rusty nail to the foot can cause infection, infection can cause gangrene, gangrene can run through the body, and rampant gangrene can cause death. All from one rusty nail. But it was the pain that alerted me to the problem.

Pain is one of God's best creations. It is an essential tool to help us realize something is wrong and needs correction. It can be ignored momentarily, but there reaches a point where pain must be addressed.

A Dual View

If we have any desire to advance God's kingdom, we must constantly have our eyes in two directions. First, we must look at the kingdom of this world. My wife often asks me why I read the newspaper, listen to the news (even to commentators I disagree with), and study current culture. My rationale is that I need to know what is happening around me. It is affecting me and those to whom I minister, and I must be current in my awareness, assessments, and applications. It is the context in which the work of God is being applied. I need to be, in some measure, a student of man—who he is, how he's wired, what he thinks, and the outcomes that result from his choices in this world.

But without another view our evaluations will be horribly skewed. We must also look around us in the heavenlies (where we are seated with Christ)[1] to see the kingdom of our God. Since our conversion to Christ, we have dual citizenship in both of these worlds and the capacity to see both. God gives us His Word and His Spirit to impart to us all the understanding we need of each kingdom as we commune with Him. Without this heavenly commentary we are overwhelmed. And His diagnosis and prescriptions for this fallen world are the only accurate source of truth that brings healing.

If we maintain this dual vision, we become like "the sons of Issachar, men who understood the times, with knowledge of what Israel should do."[2] Not only do we become a credible source of information on why things are happening, we can also predict where they are headed because we understand the ways of God. And, most importantly, we can give help to those around us about what must be done to advance God's kingdom. We can discern what God is saying to us. We become prophets to our age, and there has never been a season when prophets were more needed.

God's Predictable Pattern

As we gaze in two directions, we see that God always brings pain when necessary. He calls to us when we run from Him. It is an act of His love and a means of His grace. The judgments of a perfect God are always exactly right. He never applies them if not needed, and He never applies them in ways that are incorrect. His acts of judgment to a life, a church, or a nation alert us to what is wrong and needs correction.

Sometimes He dispenses judgment by simply allowing us to have what we want. He gives us over to our own choices, thus allowing never-to-be-forgotten illustrations of the futility of uninspired desires and unsurrendered directions. Romans chapter 1 describes this downward spiral. Pain always ensues from merely humanistic choices because "there is a way which seems right to a man, but its end is the way of death."[3]

Often God's judgments are more active. He intervenes by any means He deems necessary, all without sin and without committing any evil. As the Sovereign King of the universe, He has everything at His disposal. Even rulers can be used to accomplish His purposes. He hardened Pharaoh's heart and later stirred Cyrus's spirit to bring judgment and relief. The writer of Proverbs reminds us that "the king's heart is like channels of water in the hands of the Lord; He turns it wherever He wishes."[4]

We tend to look at natural phenomena from a merely world-centered view. But when we peer into heaven to see reality, we discover that even the natural elements are all in His hands.

> *From the breath of God ice is made, and the expanse of the waters is frozen. Also with moisture He loads the thick cloud; He disperses the cloud of His lightning. It changes direction, turning around by His guidance, that it may do whatever He commands it on the face of the inhabited earth. Whether for **correction**, or for His **world**, or for **lovingkindness**, He causes it to happen.*[5]

If we choose the shortsightedness of a merely lateral view, we see nothing, learn nothing, and adjust nothing. But what if we would take any current political or weather phenomena and set it in the context of the Old Testament? How would it read? What would God be saying? And what should be our response?

It's fascinating that one of our most oft repeated verses about revival involves natural disaster and financial downfall when seen in its context.

> *If I shut up the heavens so that there is no rain, or if I command the locust to devour the land, or if I send pestilence among My people, and My people who are called by My name humble themselves and pray and seek My face and turn from their wicked ways, then I will hear from heaven, will forgive their sin and will heal their land.*[6]

The Purpose of Pain

"We can ignore even pleasure. But pain must be attended to. God whispers to us in our pleasures, speaks to us in our conscience, but shouts in our pains: It is His megaphone to rouse a deaf world."[7]

The One who made us knows us. He understands what it will

> **REALITY #3**
> **THE PAIN WE NEED:** *God's judgments are His necessary tools to bring us to desperation.*

take to bring us to repentance. And He knows that it will often take pain. His judgments are not evil, but essential and good, and we can turn to Him anywhere along the cycle of spiritual awakening. When we see His judgments to our nation, we should rejoice that He loves us enough to do that which will bring us to repentance. We must ask Him what He is saying and be bold to proclaim it to those around us. And then we must quickly adjust to His plans.

He is seeking to bring us to the desperation that is a part of genuine repentance —the godly sorrow that leads to "repentance without regret."[8]

We've all had those moments . . . moments when we knew what we were doing was wrong and made a halfhearted turn. But in our souls we still loved our sin. Real repentance involves seeing our sin as God sees it and agreeing with His assessment. It involves a Spirit-wrought grieving. God even commands us to "be miserable and mourn and weep; let your laughter be turned into mourning and your joy to gloom."[9] When we get to such depths of desperation we are willing to turn with no reservations. And this is a turning that lasts. God knows this and it is His mercy that sends judgment that leads to repentance.

When the Shield Is Down

What would happen if God removed His hand of protection from us? All hell would break loose.

We all remember the tragedy of 9/11. God did not cause this moment (He is not the author of evil)[10], but could it be that

God was removing His protecting hand? In our arrogance we have paid little attention to Him. Killing one million babies a year, breaking our marriage covenants at record rates, endorsing and applauding all kinds of moral perversions, abusing the stewardship of the finances He has entrusted us as we spend it all on ourselves and plunge into insane levels of debt, and most tragically, being a church that misrepresents God are all overwhelming indictments. Our pride and prejudice abound. Worst of all, His bride, the Church, is ignoring His calls to repentance.

If we understand the Bible and the holiness of our great God, how could we not expect judgment? Could it be that 9/11 was God allowing us to see what full-blown evil looks like when we reject Him? When we fail to live under His leadership and continually choose our own selfish agenda? When our greatest concern is our economy and not His glory?

> THE GREAT TRAGEDY OF 9/11 IS NOT ONLY THE HORRIFIC LOSS OF LIFE, BUT THAT THERE WAS ONLY A MOMENTARY FLURRY OF SPIRITUAL RESPONSE.

The great tragedy of 9/11 is not only the horrific loss of life, but that there was only a momentary flurry of spiritual response. The churches were filled the month following the tragedy. But soon attendance dropped to levels lower than before the tragedy.

God is trying to get our attention. His judgments are the megaphone to shout to us. How bad does it have to get before we listen?

A Question from Around the World

During a Forum on Revival at the 2011 Moody Pastors' Conference, a visiting pastor from Uganda asked if he could share a comment and then ask a question. He told of the godly people of Uganda who had prayed for revival. God sent it in dramatic fashion, but it required devastation first. Their nation suffered horrible atrocities.

After describing the amazing results of revival, he said they have now turned their prayers toward America. They are asking God to send an outpouring of His Spirit to our land, knowing it would impact the world. He said the leaders know that God will send revival . . . and that it will either come through desperation or devastation.

Then came the question: "What are you, as Christian leaders in America, going to do to foster a spirit of desperation so it does not require devastation?"[11]

God is speaking. Now. Are we listening?

THINKING IT THROUGH

1. What have you seen in America in the last ten years that might be signs of God's judgment upon our nation?

2. The "remedial" judgment of God is that which is sent to correct us, and there is hope of change. The "final" judgment of God means that there is no possibility of escape. Do you see our nation under God's remedial judgment or final judgment? And why?

3. Take a moment and read 2 Chronicles 7:13–14. Read all of it carefully. What do you think this is saying to us right now as a nation?

4. If God sends judgment to our nation, who is responsible for that happening (according to the verses above)?

5. Read Habakkuk 3:2. What do you think this verse means, and what application does it have for us today?

CRYING OUT!

Spend an extended season in prayer around the following themes:

Thanksgiving:

- Thank God that He loves us enough to speak loudly to us when we need to repent.

- Thank God for His judgments. Acknowledge all the ways you see that they help us and that we need them.

Intercession:

- Spend time praying for God's mercy. Pray through Psalm 80 verse by verse and let the psalmist's prayer be your prayer from your heart.

- Think through every sign of judgment that you see in our nation and cry out to God for His mercy, and plead with Him for forgiveness for our national sins.

REVIEW—Revival Realities:

1. It's About Him: *A spiritual awakening is the visible invasion of the King and His kingdom.*
2. It Starts Here: *National awakenings begin with personal reviving.*
3. **The Pain We Need: *God's judgments are His necessary tools to bring us to desperation.***

Watch the accompanying video to Reality 3 and download additional resources at www.OneCryBook.com/reality3.

HE'S LISTENING

I love the Lord, because He hears my voice and my
supplications. Because He has inclined His ear to me,
therefore I shall call upon Him as long as I live.
The Psalmist
Psalm 116:1–2

think it developed because we have eight children. Not sure. But somewhere along the way I learned the manly, nighttime art of playing possum. If you're a dad, you are nodding your head in agreement.

It's 3:00 a.m. You've had a long day. Staying up late, you finally fall asleep in your recliner and later lumber to your bed like a hibernating bear for a long winter's nap. Suddenly, a faint cry of your newborn child creeps into the edges of your consciousness. "Is it a dream? Is there an alien in the house? Could a child really cry that loud? Is there some response needed? Why is this interrupting my precious sleep?" And the most important question: "Who will move first?"

As it persists, you recall that, yes, you do have a child and, yes, he is crying. And then the sleep-shattering realization that, yes, you are one of the parents who birthed this crying wonder.

Then the moment of decision: "Do I get up and help with the little crumb-grabber and 'love my wife like Christ loved the church and gave His life for her' or do I keep my eyes shut and body motionless, pretending to be in Level 4 sleep (i.e., assuming the possum position)?"

But there's one who cannot ignore that cry. It's inbred in a mother to hear the desperation of her children. She can hear their cries through the night, through her sleep, in a mall, in an auditorium when her child is in the nursery. It's uncanny. This precious attentiveness is motivated by a God-given love and nurtured by nine months of attachment in the core of her being. She knows that babies cry when there is a need and she will meet that need, whether she gets help from the possum sleeping next to her or not!

God's Startling Desire

Of all the amazing attributes of God, perhaps the most endearing is His willingness to commune with us. God has chosen to make Himself known to His children. He speaks to us and allows us to address Him. Made possible by a matchless introduction through the blood of His Son, we can now have peace facing God.[1] Not only does He allow us in His presence, He longs for His children to be there. He delights in us. He who knit us together in our mother's womb and birthed us again unto Himself through the cross and regenerating work, hears our cries. It's unfathomable to us that such attraction could be there, but then we have never known perfect love like this before.

"Call to Me," He says, "and I will answer you, and show you great and mighty things, which you do not know."[2] He wants to reveal to those He loves "things which eye has not seen and ear has not heard, and which have not entered the heart of man."[3] He invites us to ask big prayers—mountain-moving requests—and test Him to prove to the world His magnificence. He hears our prayers when we are in crisis, when we are interceding for the needs of those around us, or when we simply long for a long conversation throughout the day. Andoniram Judson, the faithful missionary who served in Burma for six years before he ever saw one convert, said, "I never prayed sincerely and earnestly for anything but it came at some time; no matter at how distant a day, somehow, in some shape, probably the least I would have devised, it came."

Our Helper

There are times when our weakness or burden overwhelms our ability to pray. When the weight of a lost friend, a lost child, or a lost world buries us in despair. But God does not leave us helpless. He has sent His Spirit to reside in us so that we will have the ability to cry out in ways even beyond our reach.

> In the same way the Spirit also helps our weakness; for we do not know how to pray as we should, but the Spirit Himself intercedes for us with groanings too deep for words; and He who searches the hearts knows what the mind of the Spirit is, because He intercedes for the saints according to the will of God.[4]

REALITY #4
HE'S LISTENING: Your humble cry makes a difference!

If we would pursue Him in prayer, we would discover that He has given us everything needed to become mighty in the one thing that moves heaven and earth above all else. Like a mother with her child, God hears the cries of His children. And these cries can do whatever God can do, for prayer is connecting and cooperating with Him. We cannot, of course, manipulate God in prayer. It is just the opposite.

In prayer we find ourselves aligning with Him so that His desires become ours. In such agreement, He allows us the blessed privilege of being involved in that which makes His kingdom come and His will be done on earth as it is in heaven.

God is listening, the Spirit is empowering, the world is dying and needs the effects of our intercession. Will He find us praying?

Unclaimed Treasure

The Scriptures shout to us with exhortations and examples of how faithfully God hears and answers the cries of His children. James reminds us of a man who prayed and the sky withheld rain for three years, then prayed again and the sky poured forth rain. We would think this was some unique aberration in history except for the fact that James reminds us Elijah was a man "with a nature like ours."[5] If God heard Elijah's prayers, he can hear yours.

James gives us this faith-building promise: "The effective prayer of a righteous man can accomplish much."[6] God is reminding us to think big. He can and will accomplish things—mighty things—and not just a few things, but "much!"

J. Hudson Taylor left the shores of England to start a new mission work in China in 1853. Mightily influenced by his friend and colleague, George Mueller he set out to illustrate what God could do in response to prayer. In the next fifty-two years the China Inland Mission was developed. When he laid down its leadership, it had 849 missionaries, 1,282 native workers, 205 stations, 632 sub-stations and 35,726 communicants, 188 schools with nearly 3,000 pupils, and 44 hospitals and dispensaries.[7]

"The prayer power has never been tried to its full capacity," Taylor said. "If we want to see mighty wonders of divine power and grace wrought in the place of weakness, failure, and disappointment, let us answer God's standing challenge, 'Call unto me, and I will answer thee, and show thee great and mighty things which thou knowest not!' "[8]

Do you think God could send revival to your church, your city in response to your prayers? Kitty Longstreth did.

In 1972, Kitty attended a conference where the founder of Campus Crusade for Christ, Bill Bright, was speaking. He challenged the crowd to go home and pray for the people of their city. Miss Kitty, as she came to be called, took Bright literally. She tore up the phone book of Little Rock, Arkansas, handed it out to a small band of praying women, and they began to intercede every Monday, name by name, for the citizens of Central Arkansas.

After several years, they realized that they needed the pastors of the city to join them in prayer. But how could this be accomplished? They were just a small band of women. And so, they prayed.

One year later, the mayor of the city revealed that Little Rock had the third highest murder rate in America. He called for every sector of the city to help. As a believer, he petitioned the pastors' aid. Soon twelve pastors gathered and began to pray monthly. That group grew to twenty-five and then fifty men. Annual Pastors' Prayer Summits began, fueled by monthly pastors' prayer gatherings. Quarterly city-wide prayer gatherings started—embryonic, but strong. In the last fifteen years, over 250 pastors and churches have been involved, to one degree or another, in a mutual passion to reach their city for Christ.

The Barna Research Group reported that Little Rock has the highest percent of evangelicals of any major city in America (22%).[9]

Miss Kitty died on March 21, 2012, at ninety-three years of age. The week before her death, she was meeting with her prayer group, crying out for her city, which she had faithfully done for forty years.

I wonder who met her at heaven's door, and I wonder what His evaluation was of the effectiveness of her prayers?

Jonathan Edwards said, "There is no way that Christians in a private capacity can do so much to promote the work of God and advance the kingdom of Christ as by prayer."[10]

God hears your prayers . . . and they matter.

Does It Make a Difference?

Our struggle is—isn't it?—to achieve and retain faith on a lower level. To believe that there is a Listener at all. For as the situation grows more and more desperate, the grisly fears intrude. Are we only talking to ourselves in an empty universe?[11]

The great enemy of God's kingdom loves to create questions in our minds about prayer, but on his part he trembles when humble believers cry out to God. He understands that God is sovereign and brings reviving in His own seasons and ways, but there is no doubt that he must also know that God has pledged Himself to hear the cries of a single, humble, persistent believer! Why else would Satan so oppose us in prayer? Why would he provide every temptation to us to busy ourselves with that which does not matter, diverting us from the throne of grace and power?

And why would God Himself give so many admonitions to

persevering in prayer if there was no value there? He reminds us in Luke 18 of the widow who wore the judge out by her continual pleas. The judge finally relented and answered her. Then Jesus applied it to the perseverance of faith-filled prayers:

> And the Lord said, "Hear what the unrighteous judge said; now, will not God bring about justice for His elect who cry to Him day and night, and will He delay long over them?"[12]

And then He answers His own question and, in so doing, gives us a sure promise about the future:

> I tell you that He will bring about justice for them quickly. However, when the Son of Man comes, will He find faith on the earth?[13]

God WILL answer! He will bring about justice. He will do it quickly. He will reverse the tide. He will vindicate Himself and redeem men in the process. But He asks of us a question: "When I come, will I find you praying? Will you be in faith? Will you be trusting My promises to deliver?"

He is listening. Are you praying?

THINKING IT THROUGH

1. Do you believe God really will answer your prayer? Why or why not?

2. Share with others a recent answer to prayer you've experienced.

3. Are there any times or conditions when God will NOT answer our prayers?

4. As believers across the nation cry out for revival and awakening, do you think there is a "tipping point," when the last prayer has come, before God sends revival? If so, what does that mean to you about your daily intercession for revival?

5. What do you think you could do to increase your faith in prayer?

6. What do you think God means in 1 Thessalonians 5:17 to "pray without ceasing"? Is this possible? If so, how?

CRYING OUT!

Spend an extended season in prayer around the following themes:

Thanksgiving:

- Think of how you feel and respond when one of your children cries out. What is it about God's nature that makes Him attentive to a single believer's cry? Spend time thanking Him.

Intercession:

- Pray that you would experience personal revival and for our nation. Take Psalm 85 and pray through the psalmist's cry for revival.

- Determine before God to take the next thirty days and pray each day, in some way, for revival and awakening in our nation.

REVIEW—Revival Realities:

1. It's About Him: *A spiritual awakening is the visible invasion of the King and His kingdom.*
2. It Starts Here: *National awakenings begin with personal reviving.*
3. The Pain We Need: *God's judgments are His necessary tools to bring us to desperation.*
4. **He's Listening:** *Your humble cry makes a difference!*

Download the OneCry daily prayer guide for spiritual awakening and watch the accompanying video to Reality 4 at www.OneCryBook.com/reality4.

WAITING FOR *ONE* CRY

*There has never been a spiritual awakening in any
country or locality that did not begin in united prayer.*
A. T. Pierson

The Angers Bridge was completed in 1839 and had been used successfully for eleven years to cross the Maine River in Angers, France. No one, particularly the engineers, would have believed that it would become the site of a terrible tragedy. It happened on April 16, 1850.

In the midst of a violent thunderstorm, 486 French soldiers were walking in cadence across the bridge. The combination of the swaying of the bridge in the storm and the powerful resonance created by the lock-step of the soldiers caused the suspension cables to snap, plunging 226 men to their death.

To this day, military ranks around the world break cadence when crossing a bridge so as not to repeat this disaster.

The Amazing Power of Oneness

From the beginning of time, God has illustrated that superhuman things can be accomplished when men are moving together in unity. Early in our history, mere humanistic oneness threatened the destruction of the world so much that God created disunity at the scene of the building of the Tower of Babel.

> *The Lord said, "Behold, they are one people, and they all have the same language. And this is what they began to do, and now nothing which they purpose to do will be impossible for them."*

Genesis 11:6

Whole nations can be affected when they move in unity. I know it's hard to believe, but I can remember a time in my childhood when every street and highway in America was lined with trash. It was the common and accepted practice in the '50s to throw your trash out your car window.

WHEN MEN ARE UNITED, EITHER FOR GOOD OR EVIL, THERE IS AN INHERENT POWER.

But a campaign was begun in 1953 by a consortium of business and nonprofit groups to change the nation's collective conscience on this issue. It took several years, but soon we began to see the effects of the "Keep America Beautiful" campaign. In my elementary school, we made "Don't Be a Litterbug" posters. Amazingly, the nation became unified on this idea and an entire country's thinking was changed. Every day in America we live with the illustration of what can happen when people are united.

The united Triune God—Father, Son, and Spirit—made us in Their image. When men are united, either for good or evil, there is an inherent power in our unity.

There can be a negative power, as seen in the united disbelief and rebellion of the Israelites that caused their entire nation to wander and die for forty years in the wilderness.

> *Then **all** the congregation lifted up their voices and cried, and the people wept that night. **All** the sons of Israel grumbled against Moses and Aaron; and the **whole** congregation said to them, "Would that we had died in the land of Egypt! Or would that we had died in this wilderness!"*[1]

But there is a greater, redeeming aspect of unity. When God's people are authentically and practically in oneness with Him, they will automatically move toward oneness with other believers. It is important to note that this is not just "unity for unity's sake." It is also not simply uniting around some man-made agenda (even if it sounds spiritual). It is the organic unity that occurs when believers are in unity with Christ.

In this unity, divine power is unleashed for God's kingdom. And no one knew this better than Christ.

Jesus' Final Prayer

We can know a person's heart by what they pray. Thankfully, we are treated to the extraordinary privilege of hearing Christ's greatest prayer for us before His death. His one great burden? For the church to walk in oneness!

> *I do not ask on behalf of these alone, but for those also who believe in Me through their word; that they may all be one; even as You, Father, are in Me and I in You, that they also may be in Us, so that the world may believe that You sent Me. The glory which You have given Me I have given to them, that they may be one, just as We are one; I in them and You in Me, that they may be perfected in unity, so that the world may know that You sent Me, and loved them, even as You have loved Me.*

John 17:20–23

When Christ walked the earth, He moved in perfect unity with the Father. He explained His life by saying that He did nothing on His own initiative but simply said what He heard His Father saying and did what He saw Him doing.[2] This was so complete that He proclaimed to Philip, "Anyone who has seen me has seen the Father!"[3] His oneness with the Father created a conduit for God to be brilliantly displayed.

United with Christ

The church is the body of Christ. When we are in sync with the Head, the life, power, and direction of Christ can flow through us in superhuman dimensions. God can be clearly seen. It is one thing to see this in an individual life, but think of what would happen if a whole group of believers were genuinely and practically united with Christ and each other?

Imagine the picture that would be created and the power unleashed if the whole church in a city or nation would cooperate out of this oneness. Jonathan Edwards understood this theologically and practically and wrote a famous call to the church prior to the First Great Awakening.

"An Humble Attempt to Promote Explicit Agreement and Visible Union of God's People in Extraordinary Prayer for the Revival of Religion and the Advancement of Christ's Kingdom on Earth" had a long name and a short purpose: to unite the church in prayer for revival. This call was one of the most significant tools God used to ignite united prayer among God's people that led to the First Great Awakening.

Edwards's endgame was not united prayer for the sake of united prayer, nor even revival for revival's sake. He longed for united prayer that would lead to the reviving of the church, so there would follow the rapid expansion of the kingdom and the increased worship of Christ. A revived church, marching in sync with the Master, opens the door for great spiritual awakening among those without Him.

Edwards was biblically convinced that this must begin in a united cry. He understood what would happen if the church would *agree together* in prayer. And the First Great Awakening that followed validated his theology.

OneCry

Throughout human history, there is a predictable phenomenon that teaches us something about the ways of God. Prayerfully read aloud the following scriptures (it will take you less than two minutes) and notice the pattern. What is universally true in each of these real life accounts and instructions?

> *Now it came about in the course of those many days that the king of Egypt died. And the sons of Israel sighed because of the bondage, and they **cried out**; and their **cry** for help because of their bondage rose up to God. So God heard their groaning; and God remembered His covenant with Abraham, Isaac, and Jacob.*[4]

> *Now the people became like those who complain of adversity in the hearing of the Lord; and when the Lord heard it, His anger was kindled, and the fire of the Lord burned among them and consumed some of the outskirts of the camp. The people therefore **cried out** to Moses, and Moses prayed to the Lord and the fire died out.*[5]

> *But when we **cried out** to the Lord, He heard our voice and sent an angel and brought us out from Egypt . . .*[6]

*I brought your fathers out of Egypt, and you came to the sea; and Egypt pursued your fathers with chariots and horsemen to the Red Sea. But when they **cried out** to the Lord, He put darkness between you and the Egyptians, and brought the sea upon them and covered them; and your own eyes saw what I did in Egypt.*[7]

*And the men of Kiriath-jearim came and took the ark of the Lord and brought it into the house of Abinadab on the hill, and consecrated Eleazar his son to keep the ark of the Lord. From the day that the ark remained at Kiriath-jearim, the time was long, for it was twenty years; and all the house of Israel **lamented** after the Lord. Then Samuel spoke to all the house of Israel, saying, "If you return to the Lord with all your heart, remove the foreign gods and the Ashtaroth from among you and direct your hearts to the Lord and serve Him alone; and He will deliver you from the hand of the Philistines."*[8]

*When Jacob went into Egypt and your fathers **cried out** to the Lord, then the Lord sent Moses and Aaron who brought your fathers out of Egypt and settled them in this place. But they forgot the Lord their God, so He sold them into the hand of Sisera, captain of the army of Hazor, and into the hand of the Philistines and into the hand of the king of Moab, and they fought against them. They **cried out** to the Lord and said, "We have sinned because we have forsaken the Lord and have served the Baals and the Ashtaroth; but now deliver us from the hands of our enemies, and we will serve You." Then the Lord sent Jerubbaal and Bedan and Jephthah and Samuel, and delivered you from the hands of your enemies all around, so that you lived in security.*[9]

*They were helped against them, and the Hagrites and all who were with them were given into their hand; for they **cried out** to God in the battle, and He answered their prayers because they trusted in Him.*[10]

In You our fathers trusted; they trusted and You delivered *them. To You they **cried out** and were delivered; in You they trusted and were not disappointed.*[11]

*Then they **cried out** to the Lord in their trouble; He delivered them out of their distresses.*[12]

*The Lord has done what He purposed; He has accomplished His word which He commanded from days of old. He has thrown down without sparing, and He has caused the enemy to rejoice over you; He has exalted the might of your adversaries. Their heart **cried out** to the Lord, "O wall of the daughter of Zion, let your tears run down like a river day and night; give yourself no relief, let your eyes have no rest. Arise, **cry aloud** in the night at the beginning of the night watches; pour out your heart like water before the presence of the Lord; lift up your hands to Him for the life of your little ones who are faint because of hunger at the head of every street."*[13]

*Consecrate a fast, proclaim a solemn assembly; gather the elders and all the inhabitants of the land to the house of the Lord your God, and **cry out** to the Lord. Alas for the day! For the day of the Lord is near, and it will come as destruction from the Almighty.*[14]

Do you notice the astounding similarities?

- There was a crisis that brought people to desperation.
- They cried out together (a *united* cry).
- God, in every case, delivered!

I can find no biblical illustration—not one—of God's people crying out together in humble, desperate, repentant oneness that God did not answer their prayers! This indicates to us a pattern and a prescription. It seems that if we will unite in one cry, God will hear and give us what we so desperately need. Again, we cannot manipulate God, but doesn't this biblical pattern teach us that the very first step we must take is to cry out together to the only One who can bring deliverance?

REALITY #5
WAITING FOR *ONE* CRY: *A united cry is uniquely irresistible to God.*

There is a reason why we are joining together in OneCry across America. It is based in clear theology and verified by historical illustration. It is the same call that was the precursor to the First Great Awakening. It is a plea for united intercession for the only thing that will save us in this desperate hour: *a mighty visitation from God.*

What would happen if thirty churches in your city asked their people to cry out every week for God to send revival? If every month, on a selected day, the churches had covenanted together to meet as a church for prayer for revival? If you could go throughout the city on the first Monday of the month, for instance, to any of the thirty churches and find them praying? What if they committed to join together once a quarter and they all came together to pray? What if the entire body of Christ in America agreed together about our need of repentance? What would occur if we turned together toward Him in humility and fervency? If we interceded together for His mercy and grace?

We have some indication from the Scripture. One New Testament moment gives us insight.

One Mind

Following Christ's ascension, His faithful but fearful followers gathered and waited on the Lord and did exactly what He instructed.

> *These all with one mind were continually devoting themselves to prayer . . . .*[15]

They didn't plan, organize, or move. They united together

continually. Not for a single meeting, a one-shot encounter, but an ongoing season. They had one mind that came out of one desperation and one direction to one source. A. W. Tozer understood this:

Has it ever occurred to you that one hundred pianos all tuned to the same fork are automatically tuned to each other? They are of one accord by being tuned, not to each other, but to another standard to which each one must individually bow. So one hundred worshipers [meeting] together, each one looking away to Christ, are in heart nearer to each other than they could possibly be, were they to become "unity" conscious and turn their eyes away from God to strive for closer fellowship.[16]

And they were "devoted." This word carries the idea of being "strong toward" something. I know some men who are strong toward sports or strong toward work. These men and women in Acts were strong toward prayer. It was a recognizable reality.

This continual, united prayer led to one answer from the one God. At the perfect moment, God came in manifest power! Granted, Pentecost was a not-to-be-repeated event, as the Spirit is given now to every believer. This was the birth of a new era. But the events of this moment and the residual effects give us an indication of what happens when a group of Christ-followers come to complete oneness with God and each other.

One Voice

At the Tower of Babel (a picture of humanistic oneness), God had to confuse their tongues to prevent increased pride and humanistic ruin. At Pentecost, a moment of perfect oneness, all the believers spoke in the language of every nation under heaven and yet there was ONE MESSAGE! There was perfect unity centered around the essential message of the cross.

In the mercy drop of revival that God brought to The Summit Church in the spring of 2011, everyone—and I mean EVERYONE—was talking about Christ.

One Friday night I discovered that my college son had been out all night with some buddies in an impoverished area of our city sharing Christ. He and his friends had gone by a local grocery store around 2:00 a.m., come to our house and made sandwiches for the homeless, and gone out the rest of the night witnessing! (I know this because we found the residual effects in the kitchen the next morning!)

The next day my other son joined them. The following day, my youngest daughter became upset that we would not allow her to go to this rough area of the city with her brothers. So she and her friend went to a local store and shared Christ with twenty-two people! I thought, "What in the world has happened to my children? I can hardly get them out of bed and now I can't stop them from telling about what they've seen and heard!"

When God comes, we are overwhelmed and spontaneous with the only message that really matters.

One Power

At Pentecost, Peter stood to preach and, in one of the most amazing displays of divine might, three thousand people were instantly pierced to their heart and brought to repentance, faith, and confession. The Jerusalem church was birthed in an instant. (Talk about church planting!)

R. A. Torrey recounts this amazing story of oneness in a small town:

> Up in a little town in Maine, things were pretty dead some years ago. The churches were not accomplishing anything. There were a

few godly men in the churches, and they said: "Here we are, only uneducated laymen; but something must be done in this town. Let us form a praying band. We will all center our prayers on one man. Who shall it be?" They picked out one of the hardest men in town, a hopeless drunkard, and centered all their prayers upon him. In a week, he was converted. They centered their prayers upon the next hardest man in town, and soon he was converted. Then they took up another and another, until within a year, two or three hundred were brought to God, and the fire spread out into all the surrounding country. Definite prayer for those in the prison house of sin is the need of the hour.[17]

One Possession

When we are in sync—really in oneness—with the Father, we realize that everything we have is His. In this moment of perfect oneness, the Jerusalem believers began to hold everything in common. I don't think this was a communal system, but the clear understanding that everything they had belonged to the One who had given it, and He had the right to do with His possessions what He desired. The Jerusalem believers simply became His generous channels. They realized that God owns everything in the world, and He wants it in circulation to bless us, bless others, and honor Him.

The result of this amazing oneness was one of the greatest testimonies of the reality of God that human history has ever known. There were thousands in this Jerusalem church by the time of this account. Some biblical historians say there were over 50,000. And yet, because of the oneness that God's manifest presence brought, there was "not a needy person" in this entire church![18]

Can you envision what it would be like if this happened in your city? What if this channel of resources was opened and this generosity flowed between every church and believer? What if one group gave to another, one church to another, one individual to another? And what if it was so rampant that the world noticed that there was "not a needy person" left among the believers? Is this possible? Absolutely. In fact, it has been the norm rather than the exception in times of genuine revival and spiritual awakening.

Can you fathom the testimony this would be to a watching world?

One Lord

Could it be that the reason God waits on our *united* cry is that He longs for and demands of His creatures that they *all* look to one God? Wasn't His first commandment that we should have "no other gods" besides Him?[19] Didn't Jesus say the greatest commandment was to "love the Lord your God with all your heart, and with all your soul, and with all your mind"?[20] Hasn't God warned us that the beginning of destruction begins when God reveals Himself and we worship and serve the creature "rather than the Creator, who is blessed forever"?[21]

When His people rebel against this foundational allegiance, God waits till we join together in desperation and dependency upon Him. He will meet any individual who comes to Him. But He sends revival and awakening to nations when the whole church cries out. He is merciful to meet us in powerful reviving power as His people humble themselves and pray and seek His face and turn from their wicked ways.[22]

As Christ manifests Himself in response to our united cry, the message of Christ will be on everyone's lips, the power of God will be everywhere evident, the provisions of God will flow in stunning generosity, and the glory of God will be revealed! All flowing from a people who became desperate and were "continually devoting themselves to prayer."[23]

The amazing power of one cry.

THINKING IT THROUGH

1. Why do you think the church is in such disunity?

2. What would the people in your community who do not know God think if they heard that all the churches in your city were united in prayer?

3. God hears every single cry. Why would God respond more to a united cry?

4. What do you think could happen to move the believers in your city to unite in one cry?

5. God has used ordinary people to change nations. What could you do to help move the whole church in your city to a united cry for revival and spiritual awakening?

6. What do you think will happen if we do not unite in one, desperate cry?

CRYING OUT!

Spend an extended season in prayer around the following themes:

Thanksgiving.

- Thank God for the potential He has given us for unity in the body of Christ.

- Thank Him for the many promises He gives to us as we unite in crying out to Him!

Intercession:

- Spend time praying that God would unite every believer and every church in the city with HIM first, knowing that unity with HIM will bring unity with OTHER BELIEVERS.

- Pray through John 17, asking God to fulfill Jesus' prayer in your city and our nation.

- Ask God to move in supernatural ways to unite the people in your church and our nation in one cry.

- Pray for existing attempts and movements you may know about in your city, that God would grant them favor and produce results for His glory.

- Start a OneCry prayer group in your church or area for ongoing intercession. (Go to www.OneCry.com for tools and resources.)

REVIEW—Revival Realities:

1. It's About Him: *A spiritual awakening is the visible invasion of the King and His kingdom.*
2. It Starts Here: *National awakenings begin with personal reviving.*
3. The Pain We Need: *God's judgments are His necessary tools to bring us to desperation.*
4. He's Listening: *Your humble cry makes a difference!*
5. Waiting for *One* Cry: *A united cry is uniquely irresistible to God.*

Watch a video about the power of uniting, find resources on starting a prayer group, and watch the accompanying video to Reality 5 at www.OneCryBook.com/reality5.

BELIEVE

It is not enough to begin to pray, nor to pray aright;
nor is it enough to continue for a time to pray;
but we must patiently, believingly, continue
in prayer until we obtain an answer.
George Mueller

Pretend for a moment that your children and all the people you love the most are in London, England, and you are in America. You heard on the news that an incurable plague was sweeping across London, killing the entire population.

Also pretend that you have the cure. If you could just get to your children, you could save them. But (to make it a little more interesting) let's pretend that for some strange reason you do not know or believe that there are modern means of transportation. You don't know about planes, trains, automobiles, and ships.

Your children are dying, you have the cure, but in your mind there is no way to get to them. What would you do?

Some people would just give up. They would think that saving others even with the cure in hand is impossible. But others—maybe even you—would begin to walk. You might walk all the way to the Atlantic and even jump in and try to swim across the Great Pond. But in the end, all of your best, most noble efforts would fail, and your children would die.

Would they perish because you didn't love them? Or didn't try to reach them? Or didn't have the cure? No. All that you hold dear would die simply because there was something you didn't *know* and *believe* and *access*.

There is no question that God has sent revival and spiritual awakening in ways that have opened heaven and saved millions. But most believers do not even know this possibility exists. And, even those who know of God's ways in the past often do not believe that it is available now.

Some believers just throw up their hands and resign themselves to living in an increasingly ungodly world. Others try nobly, but their best efforts cannot possibly stem the tide.

We need to understand God's ways of correcting nations and saving millions through revival and spiritual awakening.

We need to believe and keep believing *until He comes*!

Only God Can Save Us

It doesn't take long to see that our nation is decaying from within. Following every other nation in human history, the rise of immorality, greed, and injustice are rapidly eating away at our moral midsection. No nation in history has survived such fast-growing cancer.

> **REALITY #6**
> **BELIEVE: *God can save us now!***

And the world has invaded the church with such pervasiveness that they are hard to differentiate. We mirror secular thinking and practice in almost every area of morality. The statistics are staggering as we peer inside the church at divorce, immorality, greed, abortion.

Many churches are simply dying a slow death. Over 4,000 churches are closing their doors annually. Every month, 1,500 pastors leave the ministry. There are fifty pastors leaving God's work every single day. In fact, current studies show that only one out of ten pastors who attend seminary will retire in any type of vocational ministry.[1]

There are many wonderful churches and thousands who have not "bowed the knee to Baal." But in spite of the best efforts of all the churches, nothing is stopping the moral and spiritual freefall in our nation.

What could possibly stop this catastrophic decline? The psalmist knew.

> *Will You not Yourself revive us again,*
> *that Your people may rejoice in You?*[2]

The writer is so adamant in God's unique ability to save us that he uses "You, Yourself" in the equation. No man can save us, no denomination, no government, no program, no new idea. We need the almighty, all-encompassing, life-changing, course-correcting power of God to invade our nation, reviving believers and awakening the lost.

Would it not make sense, then, to do the one thing that this God asks? To make every adjustment needed in your life to unite with others in one cry for revival and awakening?

God *Can* Save Us

It is one thing to believe that God is the only source of help. It is another step of faith to expectantly believe, and keep believing, that He will help us!

The writer of Hebrews reminds us of this necessity as we approach

God. This applies to revival as well as to every issue in life.

And without faith it is impossible to please Him, for he who comes to God must believe that He is and that He is a rewarder of those who seek Him.[3]

There are two wings to faith. First is DEPENDENCY. We must believe that God "is." Some translators change this to read "that He exists," but that is not what the text says. He IS should be the foundation of our belief. He is what? He is everything. He is wisdom, we're not; He is the reviver, He is the Source, He is life, He is the only one who can awaken the lost. He is everything we need. We must turn from dependency on our ingenuity and limited human strength and rely upon the only One who can save us.

AWAKENING IS GOD'S GLORY INVADING THE EARTH.

But also we must believe that "He is a rewarder of those who seek Him." This is EXPECTANCY. Faith believes. It "counts something as true, when it doesn't seem true, in order for it to be true," as one of my mentors, Manley Beasley, often said. Faith takes God at His Word.

The secret of the incredible results of George Mueller's life (who prayed in over $40 million dollars to take care of orphans while never mentioning any need to anyone except God) was not simply that he knew God could do things, but that he prayed and trusted without wavering until God *did* do things. He depended on God alone but also expected God's intervention and answers to his prayers. And in the process, he showed the world that God was a prayer-hearing and prayer-answering God.

In an interview a year before his death, Mueller was asked if he spent much time on his knees.

> *Hours, every day. But I live in the spirit of prayer, I pray as I walk, when I lie down and when I rise. And the answers are always coming. Tens of thousands of times have my prayers been answered. When once I am persuaded a thing is right, I go on praying for it until the end comes. I never give up!*

And he continued . . .

> *The great point is to never give up until the answer comes. I have been praying for fifty-two years, every day for two men, sons of a friend of my youth. They are not converted yet, but they will be! How can it be otherwise? There is the unchanging promise of Jehovah, and on that, I rest. The great fault of the children of God is, they do not continue in prayer; they do not go on praying; they do not persevere. If they desire anything for God's glory, they should pray until they get it.*[4]

One of those men was saved at Mueller's funeral, the other not many months after his death!

The psalmist in Psalm 85 expected God to work in such a way that "glory may dwell in our land."[5] This is one of the best definitions of awakening. It is God's glory invading the earth. God's glory is His nature, His character, His life. The heavens are constantly declaring this magnificence that changes everything.[6] The psalmist cries out, not for a temporary fix, but that God's glory would "dwell," that is, that His glory would settle down and be at home. And he was expecting that visitation for his own land. His own nation.

The results of God's glory invading a nation, as we have already seen, are breathtaking and unique. The church is revived with incredible passion, the lost are awakened with staggering rapidity, the culture is changed in ways that could never be accomplished otherwise, and the mission is rapidly advanced. The kingdom spreads.

It seems that every major missions movement in history has come out of seasons of revival and awakening. William Carey was launched from the Second Great Awakening in England. The Moravian missionary movement began with the "Moravian Pentecost" at Herrnhut with Count von Zinzendorf. This began a prayer meeting and missions movement that lasted for a hundred years.

The Haystack Prayer Meeting that led to the modern missionary advance in America happened in 1806 during the Second Great Awakening. Men such as George Mueller, Hudson Taylor, and William Booth were all men who had come from the fires of God's awakening.

My brother, Tom Elliff, the president of the largest missions agency in the world, recently said, "There is no possible way we can see the missions mandate of the American church fulfilled unless God sends a movement of national revival and spiritual awakening."

When God invades the church, our hearts begin to beat in unison with His, and we care for what burdens Him. And God's burden is for more men and women to worship His Son.

Why do you need to radically change your lifestyle to join with others in one cry for our nation? Because God *can* save us!

He Is Near!

No one can manipulate God. Seasons of revival and spiritual awakening are sent to us from the hand of a sovereign God who has a distinct and perfect purpose and "works all things after the counsel of His will."[7]

But there are things God has set in motion and ways He has chosen to operate. He is the one who commanded us to "draw near to God and He will draw near to you."[8] And Psalm 85 echoes this thought.

Surely His salvation is near to those who fear Him,
that glory may dwell in our land.[9]

The psalmist is not speaking of personal salvation because the whole context of this psalm is a plea for national revival. He is, however, reminding us of the simple fact that God's nearness is related to our reverence. And God's nearness is what revival is all about.

Is the Lord near? There are two very encouraging signs.

The first is the sense of growing desperation we are seeing in our land. One indication of this is the abundance of prayer movements currently in our nation. Only God can record the authenticity and repentance involved in those who have committed to pray. But it is encouraging, nonetheless.

Secondly, our low spiritual and moral state—and God's increasing judgment—are exactly the kinds of things that are always seen before moments of national revival. We think it has never been this way before, but J. Edwin Orr reminds us that before the First Great Awakening, conditions were so bad that women could not go out on the streets.[10] Bob Bakke, an authority on the Second Great Awakening, gives the following list of conditions that preceded perhaps the greatest awakening America has ever known in the early 1800s:

- Eight years of war
- Pirates and terrorist threats
- Bankruptcy

- Real estate collapse
- Plagues
- Enlightenment
- Social unrest
- Universalism
- French "Reign of Terror"
- Famine
- Political rancor
- Nasty elections
- Coarse sensuality
- Empty churches

God often uses such spiritual declension to wake up His true church. With the movement of His Spirit ringing the alarm, the church rises to cry out and God moves in revival and awakening.

We read the biblical and historical accounts of revival and our hearts burn. But God's history is still being written in the annals of heaven. What if the next few years recorded this account: "And all of God's people cried out together, and God sent a mighty revival in His church and awakened millions to worship Him."

We may be waiting on God. But it may be that God is simply waiting on us.

Before I Die

All of us have dreams. Some want their dream home, complete with grass and picket fence. Others would love to have their dream job or dream car or dream vacation. A good question to ask is . . . "If you could experience *anything* in the world, what would it be?"

I have a lot of dreams, fueled by a few years of experience and a passion for something transcendent. You don't want to ask me about my dreams unless you've got a full pot of coffee and a good bit of time. I'll wear you out.

But can I let you know just one? I dream of a mighty spiritual movement in this nation. Something that history would record—not just in human writing, but in heavenly records. A movement of God's Spirit that overpowers our human frailty and our silly wineskins. A breath from the throne of heaven that brings the church to magnificent renewal. Where people can't wait to get to prayer meetings and worship that lasts all night. Where no musical instrument is needed because the fullness of human voices raised in genuine praise is more magnificent than the greatest symphony.

When the thought of wasting time in front of a television is so useless to believers that it's passed over like stale bread. I dream of Acts 2. I dream of love that causes us to release every hold on our possessions in such remarkable ways that the whole church in any given city is caring for the needs of each believer so that there is literally "no more need" in the entire believing community.

I DREAM OF A DAY WHEN THE SILLY, STUPID, WORLDLY GODS WE VAINLY FOLLOW AS BELIEVERS ARE SEEN FOR WHAT THEY ARE AND GLADLY RELINQUISHED.

I dream of a national revival in God's true church where whole towns are marked by one characteristic—the manifest presence of

God. I see, from this reviving of God's church, a spiritual awakening among those without Christ. Where society and culture is consumed and transformed in a tidal wave of spiritual momentum. Where people without Christ don't have to be begged and persuaded to think about Christ but come running to God's altars to beg for mercy and cleansing. Where Sunday morning is a continuation of gatherings that have happened every single day. Where every home becomes a sanctuary; every gathering a prayer meeting; every person a testimony and a messenger of the gospel of Jesus Christ. Where the gospel becomes almighty and carries everything before it.

If you think I'm a lunatic, go ahead. But I'm not just dreaming. This is my God's desire . . . and He has done it before. Everything I've just described has happened, more than once, in American history. And our God is powerful enough to do it again. In spite of our sin and weakness and our fears and our traditions. It seems fantastical to us, but it's our lack of exposure to an experience of national revival and spiritual awakening that makes us so unbelieving.

That's ONE of my dreams and, I admit, the big one . . . and I'm not giving up on it until I die.

THINKING IT THROUGH

1. Real revival is a sovereign work of God. He does what He desires, when He desires, but He also calls us to respond. In fact, in His sovereignty there are many, many things God says He WILL NOT DO, if we do not confess our sin and turn and pray! (See 2 Chronicles 7:14.) What do you think is our responsibility to help create a culture of revival in our lives, our churches, and our nation? Think about this deeply.

2. Do you believe God CAN save us? Be honest. If not, why not?

3. Think deeply and describe to others what you dream about in terms of national revival. What would it look like and feel like? How would God be glorified and His Son lifted up? What could be the results of another Great Awakening in America?

4. What do you think the effects of such an awakening might be around the world if God visited our land again?

5. As you have read through this book thus far, what are some of your next steps to cooperate with God toward revival and awakening?

CRYING OUT!

Spend an extended season in prayer around the following themes:

Thanksgiving:
- Thank God for all that He has done in the past. Walk through the seasons of your life, and your church, and our nation, and thank Him for all His merciful, gracious works.

- Thank Him for His power and ability to bring revival now. Rehearse before Him the attributes that are His that make such a supernatural awakening possible.

Intercession:
- Spend time crying out to God for revival in our land. Ask Him to give you His heart and burden for this urgent need. Pray for this, for HIS glory and the honor of His blessed Son.

- And then ... *never, never, never give up praying until He comes!*

REVIEW—Revival Realities:

1. It's About Him: *A spiritual awakening is the visible invasion of the King and His kingdom.*

2. It Starts Here: *National awakenings begin with personal reviving.*

3. The Pain We Need: *God's judgments are His necessary tools to bring us to desperation.*

4. He's Listening: *Your humble cry makes a difference!*

5. Waiting for *One* Cry: *A united cry is uniquely irresistible to God.*

6. **Believe: *God can save us now!***

Watch the video message by J. Edwin Orr on "The Role of Prayer in Spiritual Awakening," and watch the accompanying video to Reality 6 at www.OneCryBook.com/reality6.

PART THREE

THE ONECRY HIGHWAY

What would it really take to see a widespread *movement* of revival? In the six realities of a revived life laid out in the preceding chapters, Bill showed us how our lives, families, and churches can be transformed by the presence and power of God in revival. But is it possible to work together to see revival sweep across whole regions of a country—or even an entire nation?

I was recently in Texas where there are plans to build a new, super high-speed highway to connect the major cities across the state, from top to bottom. It reminded me of words from the book of Isaiah that speak of building a different kind of super-highway—a highway for our God: "Make a straight highway through the wasteland for our God!" (Isaiah 40:3 NLT).

The prophet Isaiah references the custom of Eastern monarchs who would send messengers in advance to announce that their king was coming to visit his people. Since public roads were often nonexistent or overgrown and in dire need of repair, a group of people from the destination city would come out to clear the way.

John the Baptist applied this custom in his message about Jesus: "In those days John the Baptist came preaching in the wilderness of Judea, 'Repent, for the kingdom of heaven is at hand.' For this is he who was spoken of by the prophet Isaiah when he said, 'The voice of one crying in the wilderness: "Prepare the way of the Lord; make his paths straight"'" (Matthew 3:1–3 ESV).

In other words, John was saying, "God is coming to visit you through His Messiah, King Jesus. Remove every obstacle. Prepare a highway for God."

Many voices are crying out today telling us what we must prioritize: political solutions, economic solutions, educational solutions. Even moral and religious solutions. But God's number one priority is for His people to build a highway to encounter Him!

ONECRY IS A CALL FOR BELIEVERS TO UNITE IN BUILDING A HIGHWAY FOR GOD.

OneCry is a call for believers to unite in building a highway for God's presence and power across our nation, from top to bottom, and beyond. Your life can be part of a superhighway for God's presence and power! Jesus wants to visit you, your family, your church, and this nation. Is that what you want to see?

For true revival in our homes, churches, and nation, a "highway of holiness" must be built. But construction is messy, hard work! It takes dedicated builders and concerted effort to get the job done.

That's why **OneCry is calling people across North America to wake up to the spiritual emergency and to unite their prayers, their voices, and their influence to cry out to God until spiritual awakening comes.**

There is no simple formula for revival, but there are clear biblical patterns that begin with a sense of spiritual need.

STEP ONE:
Have You Awakened to the Spiritual Emergency?

OneCry is not a program, organization, or event. Instead, it's a movement of like-minded people who agree that our nation is facing a spiritual emergency and needs a dramatic turnaround—but not just the kind that comes from different politics, more education, improved morality, or a better economy. It's a plea to God for spiritual transformation of our hearts, homes, and communities by the power of the Holy Spirit.

The very first step in joining OneCry is to sign the "Declaration of National Spiritual Emergency." Making a personal commitment to what it represents is the place to begin in experiencing God's power and renewal, both personally and corporately.

DECLARATION OF NATIONAL SPIRITUAL EMERGENCY

With heavy hearts, we recognize that the church in America is in a state of spiritual emergency. Like the churches warned in Revelation, we have become lukewarm and compromised, and the light of our witness has grown dim.

We confess that despite access to more resources and biblical teaching than any other group of believers in history, we are not characterized by the supernatural power of the Holy Spirit. And we acknowledge our lack of widespread impact for Christ on our lost and disintegrating culture.

But God is waking us from our slumber and mobilizing us to pray earnestly for revival. Together, we desire to travel the narrow road of brokenness, humility, and repentance.

In desperation for God, we cry out for the extraordinary work of the Holy Spirit in our day. We believe that true revival is the only hope to reverse our spiritual recession and enable us once again to display the beauty of Jesus Christ and His gospel throughout the world.

Because we believe that only Christ can save, heal, and revive, we pledge to:

TURN: in humble repentance from every sin God reveals to us.

PRAY: with urgency for spiritual recovery and awakening.

UNITE: with other believers in spreading the hope of
Christ-centered revival.

Lord, send revival, and let it begin in me!

Name _____

Is this *your* one cry? If so, after you have signed the declaration, you can now add your name to thousands of others who have already signed the declaration at www.OneCry.com.

STEP TWO:
Will You Pray, Share, Lead?

While God uses all of us differently, I believe there is a biblical pattern in the book of Acts for how God uses people to spread His Word.

First, God calls all of us to *pray*. The believers gathered in the upper room praying expectantly for the power of the Holy Spirit (Acts 1:4–8). Second, God wants many of us to *share*. Once God's power came, the disciples spread out, raising their voices to tell others about the mighty acts of God (Acts 4:20). Third, God expects some of us to *lead*. The apostle Peter stood to address the crowds, declaring truth and giving instruction about how to respond to what God was doing. And many others used their leadership gifts to inspire, mobilize, and organize the church to reach out to the world around them.

We can find the same pattern throughout church history into our present day. In every work of God's Spirit, God wants to use people like you and me to pray, share, and lead. This is our part to play in the supernatural work of revival!

I believe OneCry will be fueled by an army of believers who will rise up to take these roles across a wide spectrum of our society. Men and women of all ages and demographic groups who will unite their hearts with one prayer, one voice, and one movement for spiritual awakening!

Can you see it?

What if thousands of prayer warriors pleaded with God for spiritual awakening? What if voices were raised sharing revival truth in communities across the nation? What if leaders called the world to spiritual renewal and laid down their agendas to partner with other leaders in issuing that call? What if believers everywhere earnestly sought the manifest presence of God?

And what if God heard from heaven and healed our land, bringing millions to Christ as in other great seasons of revival?

ONE1CRY
PRAY // SHARE // LEAD

When God was first burdening my heart with the vision for OneCry, I sensed that the tipping point for the movement would come when a specific number of intercessors, voices, and leaders activated their calling to unite in OneCry. As best I could discern, God was wanting the "firstfruits" of the movement to be comprised of 50,000 intercessors, 5,000 voices, and 500 leaders who would make the vision of OneCry the primary passion of their lives.

Perhaps God is calling you now to be among these numbers in one or more of the following areas.

PRAY / **SHARE** / **LEAD**

50,000 People Fervently Pleading with God for Spiritual Awakening

("It is time to seek the LORD until he comes." – Hosea 10:12 NIV)

Anyone who has studied the revivals of Scripture and history will tell you the same thing . . . there has never been a revival without there first being a movement of prayer. Every revival in the history of the world has been given birth to, nurtured, and/or cradled in prayer. As Matthew Henry said, "When God intends great mercy for His people, the first thing He does is to set them a-praying."

God is calling His people to prayer today in order to awaken and empower the church in revival. Prayer prepares the ground of the human heart to receive all that the Lord has for us.

The prayer of repentance deals with the sin that so often blocks the flow of the Spirit. The prayer of worship invites the Lord to come in glory. The prayer of intercession pleads with the Lord to send His transforming power. It is time to pray!

In my office I have one of only two copies in existence of the prayer requests sent in to Fulton Street during the Prayer Revival of 1857–1858. Though they were sent from all types of people, all types of vocations, and from all parts of the nation, there was one common denominator: a burning passion for God's glory!

Would you join with thousands of your brothers and sisters in Christ to pray for revival in the United States? The need in our nation is great! God is calling many to respond to this need in prayer.

Will you be one who prays?

PRAY / **SHARE** / LEAD

C | 5,000 Voices to Spread the Message

("We cannot help speaking about what we have seen." – Acts 4:20 NIV)

Imagine 5,000 bold witnesses sharing biblical truth and revival testimonies across the nation—people from all walks of life who share a vision for revival! We are trusting God to raise up many who will use their gifts of writing, speaking, sharing, singing, networking, or teaching to spread the call for revival and spiritual awakening.

In every revival, the fires spread through the power of a changed life. It is well documented that the fame of revival spreads the flame of revival. Or as someone said, "Revival spreads on the wings of testimonies." Will you carry the life-changing message of God's presence and power to those around you? Like a modern-day John the Baptist, will you help prepare the way for the Lord's coming in revival?

TELLING FRESH STORIES FUELS FRESH FAITH.

PRAY / **SHARE** / **LEAD**

 ## 500 Leaders Mobilizing God's People Regionally and Nationally

Has God given you a platform for ministry leadership? Whether you are a pastor, a denominational or regional ministry leader, or a marketplace leader in your community, God may use you to mobilize His people toward repentance, revival, and renewal.

Leaders like this have given up on human solutions and see that our only hope is a mighty outpouring of the Holy Spirit. They have a vision to make the call to revival and awakening an integral part of their ministries—not just for a season, but *until He comes*.

OneCry exists to connect prayer warriors, voices, and other leaders in various regions so that they can either begin or accelerate the work of revival in their area. We want to empower those who pray, share, and lead to inspire their friends, churches, and communities toward revival!

God has used individuals from all walks of life to lead the way to revival. But they all had one thing in common: God's power and anointing. There is but one requirement to be used as a leader in a movement of revival. They must have the Spirit of God upon them.

You may be a pastor, a teacher, a businessman, a housewife, a student, or a child. I believe that God is calling you to be an instrument to fervently pray, share the message of revival, and lead others in your sphere of influence to do the same.

STEP THREE:
Will You Ask God, "What Do You Want Me to Do?"

For those who are a part of OneCry, there is something very important to keep in mind—OneCry is not a program or an event—OneCry is YOU and YOUR CIRCLE of relationships.

In fact, the spirit of OneCry can be summarized by a symbolic action taken with an ordinary piece of chalk with which we kneel down and draw a circle around ourselves, and then look to heaven expectantly and pray, "Lord God, send revival, and begin it right here in this circle!"

This practice (traced back to the English revivalist Gypsy Smith) puts into action something we all know in our hearts: For any revival to sweep through our churches, or for any great spiritual awakening to blaze through our communities, the work of the Spirit must begin in individual hearts. It must begin in your heart. It must begin in my heart. The old spiritual got it exactly right: "Not my brother, not my sister, but it's me, O Lord, standing in the need of prayer."

The stories we've discovered from revival history, along with countless testimonies of God's work we've witnessed over the past four decades of ministry, give powerful evidence that revival isn't a result of human ingenuity, nor is it dependent on superstars. Instead, it often starts in the hearts of ordinary people whom God prompts to pray, repent, obey, take risks, and make sacrifices.

Revival spreads through unlikely people and unheard-of prayer warriors; through college students who counsel and businesspeople who pray; through dads who get serious about God and through children who seek Christ's kingdom with simple faith. It begins when someone somewhere gives their heart fully to the Lord—when someone falls in love with Jesus all over again.

With all of our hearts, we are praying for revival in the church (the restoration of God's glory) and for spiritual awakening among the lost (the rapid expansion of His kingdom). Could it be that you have a part to play in setting the stage for such an outpouring of the Holy Spirit? Could it be that God wants to use your life, your obedience, and your prayers?

Remember, real revival begins in God's people first. Not in their local government. Not in the schools. Not in the business district. Revival begins with people who have drawn circles around themselves and who, then, join circles with those who have or are ready to do the same in their own lives.

And Christians everywhere are taking up this challenge, becoming agents of spiritual awakening in their own circles of influence. The stories are pouring in about the creative and sometimes sacrificial steps people are taking to spread a passion for OneCry to their friends and communities. Thousands upon thousands are crying, "Lord, send revival and let it begin in me."

A family in New York drew a circle on a piece of cardboard and encouraged every member of their family to step inside that circle first thing each day and ask God to send revival to their own heart. God did. And the entire family was transformed with a passionate love for Jesus.

In Florida, church members filled a church parking lot with individual chalk circles, determined not to step inside the building until they first stepped inside the circle and prayed for personal revival. They understood the futility of asking God to meet with them as a church body if they did not first meet with God personally.

A hula hoop strategically placed in the living room became another family's circle. And a man in Texas sketched a circle on the final step outside his back door so that every time he came home from work, he had to step inside that circle, a reminder to invite God to meet with him before he met with his family.

Revival circles have been drawn and posted on YouTube. One married couple actually drew a heart-shaped circle and stepped inside it, asking the Lord to meet with them before they prayed for revival in their family and church.

And I will never forget the day I walked outside a church auditorium after preaching three consecutive services on a Sunday morning, only to discover a giant circle drawn around the sprawling church campus! These people had been crying out for their entire community, but they realized that a true movement of God must be experienced in their church family before it has an impact on their city.

Every day, believers are uniting their hearts in OneCry for spiritual awakening. For example:

- An elderly couple picked up NINE truckloads of walnuts (some 3,000 lbs.!) in order to sell them for money to invest in the One-Cry movement.

- A retired businessman from Indiana who spends the winter in New Orleans used his "vacation" visiting area pastors, talking to them personally about the OneCry movement. And his efforts in the French Quarter are paying off—he has been invited to talk about

OneCry on a local Christian radio station and has connected with a pastors' coalition of over one hundred pastors in the city!

- A housewife sent an impassioned letter to her family and friends, imploring them to join her in seeking God for revival with these words: "There is now a call going out to all Christians throughout our nation—a Nationwide Call for Spiritual Awakening called OneCry. . . . Oh, dear brothers and sisters, please join with us in praying for revival in your own life and the lives of your family, for your church, for our nation to turn back to God."

- An accountant wrote personal letters to several national ministry leaders, introducing them to OneCry and encouraging them to participate.

- A couple took a trip out of state to visit friends in a church they had previously attended. They spent the entire Sunday school hour sharing in a class about OneCry. They noted, "As we shared, I could see the face of an elderly woman who was on the edge of her seat. Her eyes danced with excitement. At the end she prayed and—oh, my goodness, she prayed!!!"

- A Michigan man was introduced to OneCry, became deeply burdened for our nation, and initially sensed God was leading him to ride his bicycle all the way to mile marker #1 in Key West, Florida. His goal . . . to stop at every town the Lord prompts him to stop at and pray for revival. He wants to cover America in prayer, and he wants to do it in a sacrificial way.

In these and thousands of other ways, ordinary people are spreading the OneCry call. (See Appendix 1, "Stories That Stir.")

There Is No Limit to What God Can Do

In closing, I encourage you to open your eyes to what God is doing and what He can do, as we seek Him. As we bear the consequences in our culture of the sins we commit, as our families and communities suffer under the burden of wickedness, it could be that God would use all of this to call us back to Himself. The crisis situations we find ourselves in could actually be our invitation to tear down the "idols" we've built, and turn instead to Christ, our rightful King! I believe that God desires to send this kind of spiritual renewal here, to us, to America. If only we'll ask. If only we'll repent. If only we'll seek His face, and set our hearts toward His kingdom.

Author Dave Keesling put it this way: "The gospel's simplicity is its ability to, in a single moment, change literally everything."

A. W. Tozer echoed this belief in the reviving power of the Holy Spirit in an article he entitled, *There Is No Limit to Revival*:

> *There is no limit to what God could do in our world if we would dare to surrender before Him with a commitment that says, "Oh God, I hereby give myself to You. I give my family. I give my business. I give all I possess. Take all of it, Lord—and take me! I give myself in such measure that if it is necessary that I lose everything for Your sake, let me lose it. I will not ask what the price is. I will ask only that I may be all that I ought to be as a follower and disciple of Jesus Christ."*
>
> *If even 300 of God's people became that serious, our world would never hear the last of it! They would influence the news. Their message would go everywhere like birds on the wing. They would set off a great revival of New Testament faith and witness. God wants to deliver us from the easygoing, smooth and silky, fat and comfortable Christianity so fashionable today.*

Yes, there is no limit to what God can do through revival. But God must be sought. He is calling people who see the spiritual emergency and will turn, pray, and unite until He comes in revival and spiritual awakening.

Thousands of others have made this OneCry the cry of their hearts and the organizing principle for their lives. Only one question remains: will you?

THINKING IT THROUGH

1. We hope that over the last eight weeks, your faith has grown in God's ability to send revival and awakening across our nation. On a scale of 1–10 (10 being the most) how much faith do you have that God can do this again? Explain.

2. Share your understanding of what revival really is and the difference between revival and spiritual awakening.

3. How important is your personal spiritual condition to a movement of nationwide revival?

4. What adjustments have you already started to make in your life to more fully cooperate with God in revival? How far in the circle of surrender are you?

5. What further adjustments do you need to make to have your feet (and heart) firmly planted in the center of the circle of surrender?

6. What can you, as well as your church, do to persevere in the cry for revival? What are practical steps that you can continue to take to fan a united cry for revival in your life? Your church? Your city? Our nation?

7. What is God saying to you right now about your ongoing pursuit of Him and His work of revival?

CRYING OUT!

Spend a season in prayer around the following themes:

Thanksgiving:

- Give thanks for what God has taught you in the last eight weeks.

- Give thanks for God's ability and proven history of faithfully sending revival when His people return to Him.

- Thank God that He has given us His Word and prayer as a means of communing with Him about such critical issues. Thank Him that He hears and answers our prayers and holds true to the promises of His Word!

Intercession:

- You should be better equipped to pray for revival and spiritual awakening than ever before. Take the next moments and CRY OUT with all your heart for this urgent need!

- Ask God to show you—personally and with others—how you can continue to fan the flame of revival in the coming months.

- Read through Isaiah 64 and personalize it in prayer—praying it back to God as your prayer unto Him.

Join the OneCry movement and find stories of how believers are taking action through citywide gatherings, prayer meetings, cycling trips, and more at www.OneCryBook.com/part3.

EPILOGUE

YES, I WILL...
NOW WHAT?

If you responded, "Yes, I will," and you are ready to unite with others who have said, "Yes, I will," you may be asking, "Now what?" or "For how long?" When people ask, "When will OneCry end?" I kindly reply, "When historians can record that God visited our nation in another Great Awakening."

Until then, the following points will help you make OneCry a dynamic, ongoing part of your daily life:

Will You PRAY for an Awakening?

Pray daily for spiritual awakening — Join thousands of others who pray faithfully and fervently for an outpouring of God's Spirit! On a daily basis, you can seek God's help for personal revival, church-wide renewal, and even national spiritual awakening.

Visit or start a prayer group — There are likely scores of prayer groups already meeting in your community—some in churches, others in homes, and others among friends who agree that revival is the key need of the hour. You could plug in and pray, or, if God leads, start your own prayer group.

Commit to a rhythm of prayer — The National Prayer Accord, a rhythm characterized by the consistent, united, and passionate prayers of God's people, was used to ignite great movements of revival in our nation's past. We encourage you to adopt The National Prayer Accord as a guide towards praying . . .

- DAILY as individuals
- WEEKLY as households
- MONTHLY as a church or small group
- QUARTERLY in multi-church prayer events

- ANNUALLY as a nation (e.g. National Day of Prayer) (See Appendix 2 for Additional Prayer Patterns.)

START NOW: *At OneCry.com, we offer a host of prayer tools, day-to-day prayer guides, information on how to host church-wide or even city-wide prayer gatherings, and more. We'd love to partner with you in this most important work of prayer!*

Will You SHARE the Vision?

Share the OneCry resources — We've collected a library of resources that cast this vision of spiritual awakening—for individuals, for families, for pastors—in other words, for you. We have free downloads available that you can forward to friends, print out to share with study groups, or hand out in your city.

Invite your friends to join you in a OneCry book study — One of the best tools we have to share the message is already in your hands! Get ahold of more copies of this book, and invite some friends, a small group, or your Sunday school class to go through it with you.

Give this OneCry book to a friend (or purchase another) — Not quite ready to lead a study? That's okay — you can be a voice in spreading the call to spiritual awakening simply by handing this book off to someone in your family or church. Ask your pastor if he's read it!

Use your social media influence to spread the movement — Yes, you have influence! Your social media profiles are a great way to share how God is moving in your life. Was there a particular truth that jumped off the page at you while reading this book? Or during a time of prayer? Share it!

START NOW: *OneCry.com is where you can find downloads, book recommendations, shareable videos, social media images and ideas—and more!*

Will You LEAD Others?

Proclaim spiritual awakening — If God has given you a teaching or preaching position, use it to spread the OneCry call! Many people in your church may never read a book like this, but they will listen carefully to what you say. The church kit that supplements this book may be found at www.OneCry.com/churchkit.

Use your "platform" to be a voice for spiritual awakening — If you have influence within groups of leaders, God has given you an incredible opportunity. If your heart resonates with the OneCry message, look for ways to introduce revival and spiritual awakening as a topic of conversation, prayer, and action.

Link your ministry with OneCry — OneCry was founded as a partnership of like-minded individuals and ministry groups that hope to seek God together for spiritual transformation. If you are a chaplain, ministry director, pastor, or an organizational leader, add your voice to the call. Feel free to use OneCry materials, concepts, and even artwork (available at our site) to pass the message forward. Also, be an on-site reporter. Share stories or send us content of what is burning in your heart for revival.

Host or help organize a citywide OneCry gathering Something unique happens when churches band together to seek God's face. Have you ever experienced it? Consider hosting or helping at a citywide event for multiple churches in your community. One Cry can provide you with start-up materials.

Host a concentrated time of seeking God in your church — Life Action (the founding partner of OneCry) offers in-church ministry events that focus on seeking God for spiritual renewal. Based on the message Jesus gave to the church in Ephesus (Revelation 2:4–5), the Life Action Team can come to your church and help you facilitate a special season geared toward refreshing faith, reconnecting families, and reviving a first-love relationship with Christ. To learn more, visit www.LifeAction.org and look for local church events.

START NOW: *OneCry.com provides leadership resources ranging from sermon outlines to practical step-by-step guides for building a revival culture in your church or city. And, when you visit the site, let us know how we can personally serve you or pray for your situation.*

All the resources mentioned in this section are available at www.OneCryBook.com/epilogue.

STORIES THAT STIR

God has placed each of us in a unique context within a sphere of relationships where He has blessed us with influence. The question is, "How does God want to use me in that context to pursue the outpouring of the Spirit and the advancement of the gospel?"

One of the benefits of the OneCry community is the opportunity to learn from each other regarding how to "pray, share, and lead" for spiritual awakening. The following stories are examples of how ordinary people have been used by God to put OneCry into action. And, as a result, the flame is spreading.

OneCry in My Family

Bob and Kathy Hodorek are an ordinary retired couple from a small town in Indiana. But since finding out about the power of praying together with other believers for God's power to advance the gospel, Bob and Kathy have been caught up in a series of unexpected adventures! It all started when they decided to use their winter vacation months in New Orleans in a new way. Here is a part of their story in their own words:

> God is answering our prayers!! I want to give you a brief update on the OneCry efforts here in New Orleans; it has been one of the most exciting times in my life! Living in the French Quarter, we have developed a habit of holding hands and praying as we walk a lot of places, and God is answering in amazing and unexpected ways:

1) *I thought we would start a OneCry prayer meeting and grow it, but we found different pockets of believers already praying for revival and a very diverse and healthy Pastors Coalition, so my efforts turned toward uniting all the efforts with OneCry.*

2) *We have become good friends with an influential woman who led Women's Aglow for eighteen years and was on the organizing committee for a gathering of three hundred churches in the Superdome in the 1970s. She introduced us to a Christian leader who has a radio talk show, and after we attended Bible study in his home, he invited me to talk about OneCry on his radio show.*

3) *We have met many leaders in the city and overall have been plowing ground and sowing seed for the goals of OneCry. The most exciting has been getting to know Paul, who organizes and runs the Greater New Orleans Pastors Coalition (about one hundred churches involved, very diverse ethnically and denominationally, with mailings to an additional four hundred churches). He has an unusual burden for the unity of the body of Christ. He invited me to the Pastors Coalition Prayer Meeting that meets monthly, and it was a thrill to meet many pastors and pray together! Paul is now taking the OneCry materials to the leadership committee and announcing it at the next Coalition Prayer Meeting. He is also taking it to a nearby active pastoral group.*

I feel like we are getting ready to take off IF WE PRAY!!! I am hanging on for a ride of a lifetime and am SO THANKFUL He chose me to be involved! I am so convinced He is moving on hearts to pray because He wants to answer!

Bob and Kathy are just an ordinary couple with a burden for prayer, but God is using them to encourage prayer in hundreds of others! How could God use your marriage and family to further OneCry for spiritual awakening?

OneCry in My Church

Pastor Malachi O'Brien was stirred to lead his church to seek God for revival at a conference on revival. What happened next transformed his life and congregation:

Several weeks ago, God broke into our services in an amazing way. It is almost too sacred to mention and amazing to tell for fear of stealing credit or robbing the Glory.

After returning from Refresh (a revival conference), and the night before I was to lead Sunday services at my church, I read the bio of Manley Beasley and was completely torn inside and challenged greatly in the area of devotion, prayer, and faith. Broken over what I knew God was showing me about myself, I watched a sermon on "The Fear of Man" around 4:00 a.m. in the morning. Completely devastated, I knew what God was leading me to do.

I threw away my sermon notes for what I had planned to preach, and went to Jeremiah 2:13. Instead, I preached about my sin of pride. I confessed my insecurity rooted in pride. I opened up about attempting to be a people-pleaser and attempting to hold water in broken cisterns. No outline, not a fancy sermon. I was just broken before my people and honest about God's desire for revival in our church.

At the invitation I beheld a glimpse of God's glory. About 90 percent of our church found a place at the altar. No music, no time limits—just people crying out for revival. After people were done praying, we sat in silence in awe of the presence of God. It was sacred and I dared not to say a thing. We sat, we prayed, we cried, God was real.

*Since that time, the Holy Spirit has continued to move. We have had similar invitations every week. Church has become so much more than the music, the preaching, or even the people. **It has become a symphony of people crying out for God to move.** Our prayer meetings are intense. Faith is growing for what only God can do. People are being saved and* *transformed by the gospel. Men, women, and teens are praying.*

I said all of that to say what God has placed in my heart is a deep burden for revival. I cannot drive by a single church, in a single town, in any state and not wonder what God is doing there, and what could God do if His people sought His glorious presence? What would happen if He sent revival? What would happen if God would do something that could not be explained by anything else than Him?

Every town, big or small, I wonder and I pray. I go through Walmart and wonder what could God do. I feel despair that the majority of these people do not know Christ, and unless we see a mighty move of God, they may never come to Christ. I pray earnestly for God to rend the heavens and come down. This burden has intensified to an inferno in my soul. I wake up with it and go to sleep with it. Lord, bend me!

This is a glimpse of what God does in a church when revival comes! How could your church become a "symphony of people crying out to God" for revival?

(OneCry has prepared a resource on "Building a Revival Culture" in your church. It includes urging pastors everywhere to join thousands of other churches in preaching a series of messages on revival. Resources are available at www.OneCry.com.)

OneCry in My Workplace

Jason and David Benham are two entrepreneurs on a Godward mission! As their real estate business in Charlotte became one of the fastest growing in America, they felt a distinct call to use their marketplace influence for the glory of God.

Inspired by the great moves of God that occurred in the Old Testament when the kings joined forces with the priests to seek God, they decided to mobilize the business community to help bring together the churches of Charlotte for a day of repentance and prayer for revival called Charlotte714 (modeled after 2 Chronicles 7:14) in the Verizon Wireless Amphitheater.

The pastors in the city responded wholeheartedly to the business leaders' encouragement and offer to rent the arena, and on September 2, 2012, over one hundred churches came together at the Verizon Amphitheater for a citywide prayer and worship assembly in partnership with the OneCry movement.

An estimated 9,000 people united their hearts in turning from sin and crying out for spiritual awakening. Thousands came forward to sign a 150-foot banner version of the OneCry Declaration of National Spiritual Emergency, declaring that the ultimate answer to America's problems is not political or economic, but rather a return to the gospel of Jesus Christ.

Charlotte714 has inspired other cities to unite in similar efforts, and is just one example of how business leaders, "kings" for Christ, can lead the way to revival!

How could you use your marketplace influence to promote prayer for spiritual awakening?

(You can read more about the Benham brothers, businessmen who are turning enterprise into Christ-centered mission, by going to www. BenhamBrothers.com.)

OneCry on My Campus

What happens when the believers and Christian campus ministries on a college campus come together to believe God to ignite hearts and transform their campus?

At Montana State University, fourteen campus ministry leaders from six different ministry groups decided to find out. They came together to seek the Lord for revival in a two-day prayer summit led by Collegiate Impact, a sister ministry to OneCry, and formed an alliance called a Jericho Partnership, to work together to see "the walls come down" that are blocking God's power and presence on campus.

The results have been encouraging. Mark Gauthier, Executive Director for the US Campus Ministry of CRU, stated after visiting the campus, "I know of no campus closer to revival than Montana State University." Since Mark's observation, the work of God's Spirit has only intensified. One of the campus ministry leaders at Montana State, Seth Hedge, shares this story of what God has been doing:

> Last night, April 28, I walked into this semester's final Campus Crusade weekly meeting. There was something different about this CRU meeting: the expectancy that God wanted to move on our campus was palpable.
>
> Shortly after my arrival at the meeting, over four hundred college students packed into the sanctuary. We worshiped God, students shared testimonies of how they repented from a life of sin and started following Christ. After the band took the stage to close the night in worship, hardly a soul moved toward the doors. What ensued was some of the most joyful, genuine corporate worship I have ever experienced. This was not a typical CRU meeting, because this was not a typical year at MSU!
>
> But for me, the academic year began with a fall in the area of sexual purity. Subsequently, I felt the conviction of the Holy Spirit and confessed my sin to others. I had a new desire to make my true self known to my brothers in Christ, and immense healing followed.
>
> What I did not expect to follow were the ripple effects this would have at MSU. A few weeks after my confession, about forty male student leaders, our campus staff men, spent a weekend seeking God's purity at a

cabin retreat. Many men turned to God that night, evidenced by painful tears and public confessions. We left the weekend broken and humble before the Lord, with a new urgency to live in purity.

As the year progressed, a greater sense of joy in the Lord grew among the students. It could be witnessed at our prayer meetings, in small groups, at our weekly large group meetings, and in the testimonies of people who were coming to know Christ on our campus.

Can you imagine what could happen if students on campuses across America would experience life in Jesus Christ in such a deep, powerful, and contagious way that the entire campus would be aflame with the glory of God?

(For resources to bring believers together on campuses to seek God to ignite revival, contact www.CollegiateImpact.com.)

OneCry in My City

Revival often begins in unlikely places. That means small towns or godless cities can be the epicenter for a powerful move of God's Spirit! But who would have suspected that Reno, Nevada, of all places would be a place where believers would unite for a powerful Christ-centered movement?!

Reno is a far cry from your typical Bible Belt town. Nevada as a whole has built much of its economy on human vice, including gambling and legalized prostitution. It continues to be a city that ranks high compared to other American towns in terms of divorce and addiction to gambling and drugs.

But there has been a stirring in Reno that has the potential to drastically change the character of that town and even provide a positive example to other cities across America.

On March 2, 2013, there was a gathering in Reno of a diverse group of nearly four hundred pastors and ministry leaders who came together for the first time in many years to seek the Lord, learn about revival, pray, and see what God wants to do with their growing sense of unity.

The gathering was co-sponsored by the leading Latino, African-American, charismatic, and evangelical churches in the greater Reno area, and was based on this vision for the city from Jeremiah 33:9: *"Then this city will bring me renown, joy, praise and honor before all nations on earth that hear of all the good things I do for it; and they will be in awe and will tremble at the abundant prosperity and peace I provide for it"* (NIV).

More specifically, the goal was to bring leaders together with a common purpose of bridging the natural barriers that typically divide followers of Christ who come from different cultural backgrounds. They desire to communicate visibly to the greater community that they are ONE, consistent with Christ's prayer in John 17.

Here are the key rallying points that have brought the believers of the city together in OneCry for spiritual awakening:

- Increasing the unity of believers in our region.
- Growing in love for one another.
- Displacing the powers of darkness (this begins with repentance, both individually and for the region).

What could you do to rally believers in your area toward greater unity, agreement, and collective action in seeking the Lord for an outpouring of the Spirit?

Find resources and videos on how to build a revival culture in your church and community at www.OneCryBook.com/appendix.

ADDITIONAL PRAYER PATTERNS

Prayer Pattern: The Lord's Prayer

The people of Uganda endured over two decades of misery. First, the brutal dictatorship of Idi Amin in the 1970s was responsible for as many as 500,000 deaths. After he was deposed, the country was racked by civil war, and entire regions of the country controlled by vying warlords.

One of these warlords, Joseph Koni, terrorized the country through his practice of raiding villages and kidnapping children for his army. Young girls were raped and made child-brides while the boys were forced to watch and commit unspeakable mutilations and murders.

At the height of the suffering, believers in the country began to gather to pray in the only place that afforded protection: the swamps. A cry began to be lifted to God, and the Christians believe they prayed the oppression and darkness off of the land. Today, the dictators and warlords are gone, the country is democratic and rebuilding, and their president is an outspoken Christian.

The prayer pattern of the Ugandan believers is instructive. Based loosely on the Lord's Prayer, it has three parts.

First, prayer begins with an extended season of "hallowing" or honoring God's name. Before rushing to God with a list of requests, the idea is to cultivate a sense of God's presence by giving praise and thanksgiving. This practice helps the focus be on God, fills the imagination with the greatness and power of God, and roots everything that follows in active faith.

Second, prayer continues with a season of asking God to deliver from evil. Because we live in a fallen world where Satan is active, all kinds of darkness is oppressing our world. This darkness can be external as well as internal, corporate as well as personal. But because Jesus defeated Satan through His death and resurrection, He can push the darkness off of our lives! It is amazing to experience the relief and freedom that comes into prayer times when we ask Jesus to deliver us from specific kinds of evil around us.

Finally, prayer concludes with a season of asking for God's kingdom to become established in and through us. The kingdom of God is the sphere where what God wants is done. It is God's power, presence, and activity in action. And Jesus taught us to pray that it would be extended in our lives. In other words, the kingdom is in believers and can be established in all the places we influence. And so we pray for this to take place in specific ways and contexts in our lives.

In this way, The Lord's Prayer gives us navigational points for our prayer but remains fresh as we bring the changing content of our lives before Jesus to receive His power and transformation.

Prayer Pattern: Ask Jesus Questions

A simple but effective way to pray together is to simply include Jesus in a corporate conversation through the use of questions. The facilitator asks the following questions (feel free to add your own!), pausing to give time for the participants to respond with short prayers so that everyone can pray multiple times like a conversation:

1. Jesus, what do You want us to thank You for today?

2. Jesus, what do You want us to ask forgiveness for?

3. Jesus, who do You want us to remember to pray for?

4. Jesus, what personal needs should we bring before You?

5. Jesus, what promises do You want us to claim over our lives?

This prayer pattern is so simple that children can join in easily with adults. In fact, it's a great way to pray together as a family! And it provides a loose structure while still allowing for the changing flow of a group.

PERSONAL REVIVAL CHECKLIST

(Praying Through the Sermon on the Mount)
Matthew 5–7

Jesus' Sermon on the Mount (Matthew 5–7) clearly reveals the essential elements for personal revival. If you will live in light of these truths, you can experience daily, continuous revival. To fail to heed Christ's words will lead to fruitlessness and despair.

Carefully read each Scripture and search your heart in the light of Christ's words that they might bring you to a greater repentance and a hunger to be conformed to the image of Christ. As you proceed, circle the areas of greatest need and seek God for cleansing and revival.

Chapter 5

1. Do I have a genuine poverty of spirit? Do I recognize my own ability and the critical need for God in my life? (5:3)
2. Do I mourn over my sin? When I sin, is there a godly sorrow that leads to a repentance without regret? (5:4; 2 Corinthians 7:10)
3. Am I meek? Am I willing to be governed by God alone? Is the quality of brokenness clearly visible in my life? (5:5)
4. Am I hungry and thirsty for rightness in every realm of my life? with God? with others? in every situation, circumstance, decision? (5:6)
5. Am I merciful toward others? Do I exhibit a spirit of forgiveness? (5:7)

6. Am I pure in heart? Are my motives pure? Have I laid down other allegiances and affections that I have cherished more than Jesus? Do I have a single-minded devotion to Jesus Christ? (5:8; 2 Corinthians 11:3)

7. Do I seek to be at peace with all men without compromising my convictions? Do I make peace when it is within my power to do so? (5:9; Romans 12:18)

8. Am I standing so visibly for Christ that I am in opposition to the world, the flesh, and the devil, and, because of that, suffering persecution? Do I rejoice when men revile me and say all kinds of evil against me falsely for Christ's sake? (5:10–12)

9. Does my life create a hunger and a thirst for God in the lives of others? Am I being used of God to preserve and maintain the truth? (5:13)

10. Does my life illuminate the truth about God and man before others? Do people see my good works (the fruit of the Spirit) and glorify God? (5:14–16; Galatians 5:22–23)

11. Are there any commandments, even the smallest ones, which I do not regard as binding on my life? Am I teaching others to do the same either by expression or example? (5:17–19; Deuteronomy 8:3b)

12. Is my righteousness merely external, like that of the Pharisees, instead of coming from my heart? (5:20; 22:36–38)

13. Am I angry with my brothers? Am I guilty of calling others names, criticizing others, or wrongly accusing others? (5:21–22)

14. Is there anyone, anywhere, who has something against me whom I have not approached to seek reconciliation? (5:23–24)

15. Am I overcoming lust daily? Are my eyes focused on Christ alone as my source of satisfaction? Do I have a single-minded devotion in my marriage to my spouse? (5:27–32)

16. Do I make oaths? Do I feel the necessity to make up for a lack of integrity by assuring people that what I'm saying is really true? Do I ever fail to speak with honesty and integrity? Do I exaggerate or "stretch the truth"? (5:34–37)

17. Am I taking revenge on anyone by my words or actions? even subtly? Am I failing to love them aggressively, merely tolerating them? (5:38–39)

18. Am I giving to my enemies, loving them, praying for them, greeting them? (5:40–47)

19. Am I seeking to be "perfect" or complete in every realm of my life even as my heavenly Father is perfect? (5:48)

Chapter 6

20. Am I practicing my righteousness before men? Am I anxious to let people know, one way or another, how spiritual I am—what religious activities I'm involved in? (6:1)

21. When I give, do I make sure others know about it? Am I secretly pleased when they discover it? (6:2–4)

22. When I pray, am I anxious to impress others? Do I love to pray publicly so that others can hear me and be impressed? (6:5)

23. When I pray, do I go into the inner room of my heart and shut the door? Do I pray to my Father? Am I experiencing genuine communion and intimacy with Him? (6:6)

24. Do I use meaningless repetitions in prayer? Do I secretly think I can impress God with my many words, or long moments spent in prayer? Am I resting and depending on my own efforts and abilities to gain God's attention rather than the merits of Christ alone? (6:7)

25. Am I acknowledging and praising God in prayer? Am I hallowing His name? Am I praying for His honor and glory? Do my requests reflect a desire for His glory, not just a desire for my own comfort, pleasure, and good will? (6:9)

26. Am I aggressively praying for God's kingdom to be established? (6:10)

27. Am I praying for God's will to be done—not merely interested in my selfish desires being granted? (6:10)

28. Am I depending upon Christ alone as the source of my every need—my daily bread? Do I come to Him with every need of life? (6:11)

29. Am I consistently dealing with sin in my life, seeking God's cleansing and forgiveness? (6:12)

30. Am I praying for and depending on God's protection from temptation and deliverance from evil? (6:13)

31. Is there anyone who has sinned against me, offended me, or harmed me in

any way that I have not truly and fully forgiven? (6:14–15)

32. Am I fasting? Am I abstaining from worldly issues that cloud my spiritual vision? Have I surrendered every material thing in my life that I felt I cannot do without? that I couldn't or wouldn't give up on a moment's notice? (6:16)

33. When I fast, am I anxious for others to know? (6:16–18)

34. Do I have an over-attention to storing up material wealth? Do I own a lot of unnecessary things? Are material possessions seen as "treasures" to me? (6:19)

35. Am I so investing my life and resources that I am laying up treasures and rewards in heaven? (6:20–21)

36. Do I have anything that is a master to me other than the Lord Jesus Christ? Am I holding on to anything in my life that is causing me in some way to treat Christ and the things of God lightly? causing me to despise Christ or give Him less than His rightful place? (6:24)

37. Am I worrying about material things? about what I will eat or drink or wear? Am I worried unduly about my physical appearance? Am I exhibiting a lack of faith by worrying about anything material? (6:25–31)

38. Am I seeking first of all His kingdom and His righteousness in everything? Am I investing my life and time in eternal, kingdom business (i.e., the Word of God and the lives of others)? (6:33)

39. Am I worrying about the future on any level—worrying about myself, my family, my job, my income, my physical comfort? (6:34)

Chapter 7

40. Am I judging others in a critical, condemning, or hypocritical way? (7:1–2)

41. Am I more concerned about changing others than I am about dealing with my own spiritual deficiencies? (7:3–4)

42. Do I try to correct others without first humbly correcting myself? (7:5)

43. Am I asking, seeking, and knocking before the Lord? Am I consistently and continually looking to Him with dependency and expectation, realizing that "He is and that He is a rewarder of those who seek Him"? (7:7–11; Hebrews 11:6)

44. Am I treating others as I would desire them to treat me? Do I give others as much honor, respect, understanding, and attention as I give myself? (7:12)

45. Have I entered the narrow gate that leads to true eternal life? (7:13–14)

46. Am I wary of false prophets? Do I have such a relationship with God and His Word that I am sensitive and discerning regarding that which is really true and that which is false—not naïve and gullible regarding spiritual deception? (7:15–20)

47. Am I trusting in my religious activities to make me right with God? Am I vainly believing that external relationships alone will make me right before God? (7:21–23)

48. Am I consistently in a position to hear the Word of God? Am I listening intently to what God is trying to say to me, not merely paying casual attention? (7:24)

49. Am I actively and immediately obeying God as He speaks to my heart through His Word? Is my life being built upon God's Word through instant obedience to Him? (7:24–27)

Your sins may have put a barrier between you and someone else. Go now and ask forgiveness of those you have wronged, whatever the causes. If necessary, make needed restitution. Let nothing keep you from a clear conscience. No price is too high to pay.

Finally, determine to live in immediate obedience to the promptings of the Spirit of God and directives of His Word. Trust God to use you as a powerful instrument of revival.

APPENDIX 4

REVIVAL TWEETS

At OneCryBook.com we have assembled hundreds of quotes on revival and prayer, and we invite you to use them to share your One-Cry vision. You can become a social media voice in calling out for God's presence in this generation. We have included the following tweets as some of our favorites and to help you get started right now. And at the OneCry website, it's as easy as "click and send" for you to become a voice for true revival.

When the church really takes on the humble characteristics of Christ, that's going to lead to revival.
–Francis Chan

This nation cannot be saved unless the church is first revived. Renewing the church is the key to saving America.
–Chuck Colson

If revival depended on me—my prayers, my faith, and my obedience—would America ever experience revival?
–Del Fehsenfeld Jr.

To get nations back on their feet, we must first get down on our knees.
–Billy Graham

The church always looks like the church in the New Testament when she is in the midst of revival.
–D. Martyn Lloyd-Jones

Personal revival is Jesus in you, around you, through you, under you, over you, before you, and behind you.
–Anne Graham Lotz

As long as we are content to live without revival, we will.
–Leonard Ravenhill

Is it possible that we do not see God working in mighty ways because we don't ask Him to work in mighty ways?
–C. Hansen/J. Woodbridge

The biggest billboard for revival is a changed life.
–Byron Paulus

Revival is the people of God living in the power of an ungrieved, unquenched Spirit.
–James A. Stewart

To prepare . . . for revival is to prepare for heaven.
–William Still

The history of the Church of Jesus Christ on earth has been largely a history of revivals.
–R. A. Torrey

NOTES

PART 1 – Why OneCry?

1. Go to www.OneCryBook.com to hear a powerful prayer of anguish by the late David Wilkerson.

2. Last updated 12:12 p.m. EDT, Friday, July 26, 2013, http://www.christianpost.com/news/nearly-half-of-all-first-births-in-america-out-of-wedlock-study-says-92088/.

3. Last modified July 26, 2013 at 4:20, http://en.wikipedia.org/wiki/Incarceration_in_the_United_States.

4. Thursday, November 10, 2011, http://www.lifeway.com/ArticleView?storeId=10054&catalogId=10001&langId=-1&article=Lifeway-Research-Pastors-say-porn-impacts-their-churches; posted May 23, 2013 – 12:55 p.m., http://thecontributor.com/three-alabama-cities-top-religious-porn-lists; http://www.safefamilies.org/sfStats.php

5. http://www.usdebtclock.org/.

6. Erwin W. Lutzer, *Is God on America's Side?: The Surprising Answer and How It Affects Our Future* (Chicago: Moody Publishers, 2008), 16.

7. Richard Owen Roberts, *The Solemn Assembly* (Wheaton, IL: International Awakening Press, 1989), 6.

8. Sammy Tippit with Jerry B. Jenkins, *God's Secret Agent* (Wheaton, IL: Tyndale House Publishers, Inc., 2001), 241–49.

9. "Understanding Revival," http://www.lifeaction.org/revival-resources/revive/revival-43-1/understanding-revival/.

10. Dr. Stephen F. Olford, "The Pattern for Revival," http://www.heraldofhiscoming.com/Past Issues/1998/September/the_pattern_for_revival.htm.

PART 2 – Six Revival Realities

Reality 1 – It's about Him

1. Jonathan Edwards, *Some Thoughts Concerning the Present Revival of Religion* . . . (Boston: printed and sold by S. Kneeland and T. Green, 1742) Part II, Section 1, 91. http://archive.org/details/somethought00edwa.

2. Matthew 4:17.

3. Matthew 5:3–5, paraphrased

4. Ibid.

5. Matthew 6:10.

6. John 8:28, 26.

7. Philippians 2:9–11 ESV.

8. A. W. Tozer, http://www.goodreads.com/quotes/195434-the-reason-why-many-

are-still-troubled-still-seeking-still.

9. 2 Corinthians 11:3.

10. John 10:10.

11. Ian Murray, *Revival and Revivalism* (Carlisle, PA: Banner of Truth Trust, 1994), 20.

12. Samuel Davies, *Sermons on Important Subjects*, vol. 4 (London: 1824), 49–50.

13. Dr. J. Edwin Orr, "The Role of Prayer in Spiritual Awakening," recorded at the National Prayer Congress, Dallas, TX, October 26–29, 1976. DVD available at http://www.campuscrusade.com/catalog/The-Role-of-Prayer-in-Spiritual-Awakening.html.

14. Ibid.

15. Ibid.

16. Samuel Davies, *Sermons on Important Subjects*, vol. 4 (London: 1824), 49–50.

17. Dr. J. Edwin Orr, "The Role of Prayer in Spiritual Awakening," recorded at the National Prayer Congress, Dallas, TX, October 26–29, 1976. DVD available at http://www.campuscrusade.com/catalog/The-Role-of-Prayer-in-Spiritual-Awakening.html.

18. http://familysafemedia.com/pornography_statistics.html#important_countries.

19. Isaiah 64:1.

20. Written by William Rees (public domain hymn).

Reality 2 – It Starts Here

1. A. W. Tozer, http://www.goodreads.com/quotes/329596-a-man-by-his-sin-may-waste-himself-which-is.

2. Richard Owen Roberts, *Revival!* (Wheaton, IL: Tyndale House Publishers Inc., 1982), 16.

3. Matthew 22:37–38.

4. Revelation 2:2–3.

5. Revelation 2:4.

6. John Eldredge, *Wild at Heart* (Nashville: Thomas Nelson, 2001), 172.

7. Revelation 2:5.

8. Matthew 22:37.

9. Revelation 2:5.

10. Ibid.

11. 1 Thessalonians 5:17.

12. Acts 4:20 KJV.

13. Matthew 12:34.

14. Revelation 2:5.

15. D. Martyn Lloyd-Jones, *Studies in the Sermon on the Mount* (Grand Rapids, MI: Wm. B. Eerdmans Publishing Company, 1976), 150.

16. Bill Elliff, original composition.

Reality 3 – The Pain We Need

1. Colossians 3:1ff.
2. 1 Chronicles 12:32.
3. Proverbs 14:12.
4. Proverbs 21:1.
5. Job 37:10–13.
6. 2 Chronicles 7:13–14.
7. C. S. Lewis, *The Problem of Pain* (United Kingdom: The Centenary Press, 1940).
8. 2 Corinthians 7:9–10.
9. James 4:9.
10. James 1:13.
11. Byron Paulus, "Monday Morning Memo," June 13, 2011 (internal staff communique).

Reality 4 – He's Listening

1. Romans 5:1–2.
2. Jeremiah 33:3 NKJV.
3. 1 Corinthians 2:9.
4. Romans 8:26–27.
5. James 5:17.
6. James 5:16.
7. Clifford G. Howell, *J. Hudson Taylor: Founder of the China Inland Mission*, http://www.wholesomewords.org/missions/biotaylor7.html (copyright 2013).
8. Kirk Cameron and Ray Comfort, *The School of Biblical Evangelism* (Alachua, FL: Bridge-Logos Publishers), 280.
9. "Godless Hollywood? Bible Belt? New Research Exploring Faith in America's Largest Markets Produces Surprises", Barna Group, August 23, 2005, http://www.barna.org/barna-update/5-barna-update/173-godless-hollywood-bible-belt-new-research-exploring-faith-in-americas-largest-markets-produces-surprises#.UfWBrW3Qj1U.
10. Jonathan Edwards et al, *The Works of Jonathan Edwards, A.M.* (London: William Ball, 34 Paternoster-Row, 1839), Section III, 426.
11. C. S. Lewis, *Letters to Malcolm; Chiefly on Prayer* (Mariner Books, 2002; first published in 1964).
12. Luke 18:6–7.
13. Luke 18:8.

Reality 5 – Waiting for *One* Cry

1. Numbers 14:1–2.
2. John 5:19.
3. John 14:9 NIV.
4. Exodus 2:23–24.

5. Numbers 11:1–2.
6. Numbers 20:16.
7. Joshua 24:6–7.
8. 1 Samuel 7:1–3.
9. 1 Samuel 12:8–11.
10. 1 Chronicles 5:20.
11. Psalm 22:4–5.
12. Psalm 107:6.
13. Lamentations 2:17–19.
14. Joel 1:14–15.
15. Acts 1:14.
16. A. W. Tozer, "The Gaze of the Soul" in *The Pursuit of God* (Harrisburg, PA: Christian Publications Inc., 1976).
17. R. A. Torrey, *How to Pray as You Get What You Pray For* (Record of Christian Work, 1908), 27.
18. Acts 4:32–35.
19. Exodus 20:3.
20. Matthew 22:37.
21. Romans 1:25.
22. 2 Chronicles 7:14.
23. Acts 1:14–15.

Reality 6 – Believe

1. Bill Elliff, *Whitewater: Navigating the Rapids of Church Conflict* (Little Rock, AR: TruthInk Publications), 109–10.
2. Psalm 85:6.
3. Hebrews 11:6.
4. http://www.primitivepilgrim.com/christian-living/a-personal-interview-with-george-mueller.
5. Psalm 85:9.
6. Psalm 19:1.
7. Ephesians 1:11.
8. James 4:8.
9. Psalm 85:9.
10. Dr. J. Edwin Orr, "The Role of Prayer in Spiritual Awakening," recorded at the National Prayer Congress, Dallas, TX, October 26–29, 1976. DVD available at http://www.campuscrusade.com/catalog/The-Role-of-Prayer-in-Spiritual-Awakening.html.

ACKNOWLEDGMENTS

We confess the acknowledgments page is one page we've often skipped past when reading a book. Let's get to the real stuff, we often reasoned. To those who feel as we once did, you have never written a full-fledged book! We now read acknowledgments pages first. Bill and I have received a lot of help from a wonderful group of people. Above all, our help came from the Lord . . . our Reviver and Sustainer.

The Book of Acts — The vision of OneCry is not new. All revivals are echoes of Pentecost. And every ingredient of revival can be found in this sacred action book of the New Testament. Acts provided the impetus of the OneCry movement.

Del Fehsenfeld III is the kind of leader every leader wants in his back pocket, tool bag, and prayer closet. The editor of *Revive* magazine, Del is a master at content development and delivery. Agreeing to do a project like this without Del would have been inconceivable.

Sandra Hawkins has served as a godly single woman in revival ministry for over thirty years. Theologian and revivalist in her own right, she is also an excellent editor.

Bob Bakke, David Butts, Darryl Craft, Dan Jarvis, and James Pool were all a part of the original OneCry movement partnership. These pastors and ministry leaders helped birth this movement, and they have not stopped giving all they can to move it forward by the power of the Spirit. Thanks for modeling personal sacrifice for the mission of revival.

Aaron Paulus and the Life Action Media Team — Aaron has led the operations and media development teams for OneCry. As a high capacity, global thinker who just plain loves Jesus and his family, he and his team are young, energetic, and adventurous.

The OneCry Staff — Randy Hekman and Phillip Wilson have "signed on" to help facilitate the OneCry movement. They raise their own funding and work without accolades, wholeheartedly giving themselves to see spiritual awakening come in our day!

The Moody Publishers Team — Historically speaking, most revivals are birthed through relationships. And for the past decade, there has been a strong partnership between Moody and the various Life Action brands. These folk "get it" at the highest professional level. But their hearts get it even more. Thank you, Moody, for being the kind of ministry we can look up to, knowing your motives are pure, your prayers are genuine, and your commitment is real.

Our Families — Without our families, any task in ministry would be diminished. Our wives, Sue and Holly, are our greatest partners in life and ministry. We are so grateful that, by the grace of God, all of our children are engaged in ministry (most of them vocationally) and share the vision of revival and awakening. Our greater prayer is that we would see the next generation arise with a passion for God's glory.

ABOUT THE AUTHORS

Byron Paulus *serves as Executive Director of Life Action Ministries, the largest organization in North America dedicated solely to the mission of revival. For more than four decades, he has inspired thousands of believers to seek the Lord for widespread spiritual awakening through his writing, speaking, and leadership roles. The OneCry movement was first birthed in Byron's heart, and he currently provides strategic leadership to this expanding initiative. Byron and his wife, Sue, live in Niles, Michigan, and have three children and twelve grandchildren. For his personal revival journey, visit www.OneCryBook.com.*

Bill Elliff *is the Senior Teaching Pastor of The Summit Church in North Little Rock, Arkansas. His passion is to see both genuine revival and methodological renewal in the church—both new wine and new wineskins. He is a frequent conference speaker, writer, and consultant to churches drawing from more than forty years of pastoring and revival ministry. Bill leads the pastor emphasis in the OneCry movement. Bill and his wife, Holly, have eight children and seven grandchildren (and counting!). Visit www.OneCryBook.com to learn how Bill first experienced a powerful move of God and then became passionate about revival.*

Let It Begin In Me

ONE1CRY

A Nationwide Call for Spiritual Awakening

TURN // PRAY // UNITE

in humble repentance from every sin God reveals to us

with urgency for spiritual recovery and awakening

with other believers in spreading the hope of revival

To learn more about OneCry and to join the movement, visit

www.onecry.com

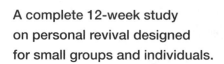